Deposit of Faith

Deposit
of Faith

HOW CAN WE MEET GOD TODAY?

—⁓—

Hubert Michael Sanders Jr. M.A.

ISBN: 0692458697
ISBN 13: 9780692458693
Library of Congress Control Number: 2015908552
Hubert Sanders, Redford, MI

This book is dedicated to my late wife, Dr. Monica Mouton Sanders. I will be eternally grateful for the great gift God gave me in her. If you are reading this, please pray for Monica's soul and feel free to ask for her intercession.

Contents

Introduction

—⁓—

THE FATHER CALLS HUMANS TO be partakers of the divine nature, which enables them to exist as creatures but more importantly as His children. Human beings, from the beginning of time, have often rejected this call. This rejection has caused the separation between God and human beings, yet the Father has ceaselessly drawn humans back to Himself through sacred kinship bonds known as covenants.[1] God's intervening presence in the world is marked by covenants, and it culminated in the coming of God's own Son, Christ Jesus. Jesus, the Second Person of the Trinity become man, came to restore what Adam lost for the entire human race. Through Jesus's perfect obedience to the Father and His death and resurrection, the human debt was paid, and a way back to the Father was created. To facilitate this return

1   cf. Scott W. Hahn, *Kinship by Covenant: A Canonical Approach to the Fulfillment of God's Saving Promises* (New Haven, London: Yale University Press, 2009), 31.

journey, Christ sends the Holy Spirit so that Christ's life may be reproduced in the lives of all human beings. It is only in Christ that communion with God is reestablished.

Jesus established the Catholic Church to unite human beings with Him. The Church is the mystical body of Christ. Jesus promised to be with His Church until the end of time (cf. Matt. 28:20). Jesus gave this promise immediately after his command to His apostles to teach everything He has commanded (cf. Matt. 28:20). The content of this divine teaching has been commonly referred to as "the deposit of faith." It can be safely assumed that this deposit of faith will play a critical role in fulfilling Jesus's promise to be with the Church. The nature and role of the deposit of faith in the life of the Church are very significant aspects of Christianity, and they are worth exploring.

This thesis will investigate the meaning of the deposit of faith as expressed by Vatican II and postconciliar documents. It will then examine the importance of the deposit of faith for Catholic life and doctrine. In order to fully understand how the terms "deposit" and "deposit of faith" are used in Vatican II and postconciliar documents, their usage in Scripture, the early Church, and encyclicals and councils that precede Vatican II need to be analyzed.

CHAPTER 1

Sacred Scripture and the Early Church

—⚊—

THIS CHAPTER WILL EXPLORE THE use of the phrase "deposit of faith" or "deposit" in the Sacred Scripture and by the early Church Fathers and as well as other early Christian writers. Sacred Scripture is the "soul of theology"[1] (DV 24), and it only makes sense to begin our theological investigation there in discovering the reality of the deposit of faith.

The concept of the deposit of faith is receiving a renewed emphasis in the twentieth and twenty-first centuries. It is also deeply rooted in Sacred Scripture. In a pastoral letter, St. Paul exhorts Timothy, a leader in the Church, "to guard what has been entrusted to you" (1 Tim. 6:20a).[2] The phrase "has been entrusted" translates the Greek word παραθήκην or *paratheken*, which literally means "deposit or trust"

---

1   cf. Catholic Church, *Vatican II Documents* (Vatican City: Libreria Editrice Vaticana, 2011), *Dei Verbum* 24.

2   Scripture quotes will be taken from Revised Standard Version: Catholic Edition unless otherwise stated.

in the legal sense of leaving an object in another's keeping.[3] The English Standard Version translation of the Bible translates 1 Timothy 6:20a as follows: "O Timothy, guard the deposit entrusted to you." This verse concludes Paul's first letter to Timothy, so in order to grasp the contents of this "deposit," a general look at the entire letter will be extremely helpful.

The verb form of *paratheken* is *paratíthēmi*,[4] which is used in the earlier portion of the letter: "This charge I *commit to* you, Timothy, my son, in accordance with the prophetic utterances which pointed to you, that inspired by them you may wage the good warfare" (1 Tim. 1:18, emphasis added). What "charge" is Paul referencing? Several verses earlier, Paul states, "As I urged you when I was going to Macedonia, remain at Ephesus that you may *charge* certain persons not to teach any different doctrine" (1 Tim. 1:3, emphasis added). Paul is urging Timothy to be a guardian of orthodox doctrine. This doctrine or teaching is founded on and in accord with the "Gospel" with which Paul has been entrusted and has the aim of love (cf. 1:11, 1:5). Paul tells the Corinthians that the Gospel, or good news, is the

---

3   Kittel, Gerhard, Gerhard Friedrich, and Geoffrey William Bromiley. Theological Dictionary of the New Testament. (Grand Rapids, MI: W.B. Eerdmans, 1985). 1179.

4   James Swanson, *Dictionary of Biblical Languages with Semantic Domains: Greek (New Testament)*, electronic ed. (Oak Harbor: Logos Research Systems, Inc., 1997).

death and Resurrection of Christ Jesus (cf. 1 Cor. 15:3–5). One aspect of this deposit (1 Tim. 6:20) being entrusted to Timothy is solid and faithful teaching rooted in faith (cf. 1 Tim. 1:4). Given that this teaching finds its source in the Gospel, which is an event that gives power, sound doctrine is not simply informative but performative.[5] Timothy must guard this deposit to protect against people departing from the faith. The mystery of the Christian faith is Jesus being incarnated, resurrected, proclaimed, and believed in (1 Tim. 3:16).

Another aspect of this deposit that Timothy must guard is morality. Timothy is encouraged to wage the war of holding faith and a good conscience (1 Tim. 18–19). Keeping a clean conscience is described throughout the letter. Paul charges Timothy "to keep the commandment unstained and free from reproach until the appearing of our Lord Jesus Christ" (1 Tim. 6:14). There is a way of behaving that Paul is trying to get across to Timothy. Greed is to be avoided, and righteousness, godliness, faith, love, steadfastness, and gentleness are to be pursued (cf. 1 Tim 6:11).

The liturgical life is another aspect of this deposit that Timothy is responsible for keeping. Paul urges Timothy "that supplications, prayers, intercessions,

---

5   Pope Benedict XVI, *Jesus of Nazareth: From the Baptism in the Jordan to the Transfiguration* (Ignatius Press, 2008), 47.

and thanksgivings be made for all men" (1 Tim. 2:1, RSVCE). Characteristics of bishops and deacons are described in chapter 3. Timothy must not neglect his office, and he must also "attend to the public reading of scripture, to preaching, to teaching" (1 Tim. 4:13; cf. 1 Tim. 4:14).

From a brief look at the whole letter, the content of this deposit primarily refers to doctrines or articles of faith. The outline or structure reveals the following:

I.   Address (1 Tim. 1:1–2)
II. *Sound Teaching (1 Tim. 1:3–20)*
III. Problems of Discipline (1 Tim. 2:1–4:16)
IV. Duties toward Others (1 Tim. 5:1–6:2a)
V. *False Teaching and True Wealth (1 Tim. 6:2b–19)*
VI. Final Recommendation and Warning (1 Tim. 6:20–21)[6]

The letter begins and ends with references to teaching. *A Catholic Commentary on Holy Scripture* comments on 1 Timothy 6:20: "that which is committed"—the *deposit* of faith. Timothy is warned to guard the treasure of sound doctrine, which, as a sacred trust, has

---

6 Confraternity of Christian Doctrine. Board of Trustees; Catholic Church. National Conference of Catholic Bishops; United States Catholic Conference. Administrative Board, *The New American Bible: Translated from the Original Languages with Critical Use of All the Ancient Sources and the Revised New Testament* (Confraternity of Christian Doctrine, 1996).

been committed to his keeping. He must shun those travesties of true teaching that led others to fall away from the faith.[7] The *paratheken* also includes references to morality and liturgical life. The deposit is seen as very valuable and worthy of protection due to the fact that salvation is at stake: "Take heed to yourself and to your teaching; hold to that, for by so doing you will save both yourself and your hearers" (1 Tim. 4:16). This deposit includes the words of our Lord Jesus Christ (cf. 1 Tim. 6:4), and the Word of the Lord is truly nourishing (cf. Matt. 4:4).

Paratheken is also used in Paul's second letter to Timothy: "[A]nd therefore I suffer as I do. But I am not ashamed, for I know whom I have believed, and I am sure that he is able to guard until that Day *what has been entrusted* to me...guard the truth *that has been entrusted* to you by the Holy Spirit who dwells within us" (2 Tim. 1:12, 14, emphasis added). Paul has been entrusted with the responsibility of preaching the Gospel (cf. 2 Tim. 1:11). The deposit given to Timothy is not only the Word of Christ but also the truth given by the Holy Spirit. This Gospel truth is intended to be passed on to other generations as indicated in the following verse: "[A]nd what you have heard from me before many witnesses *entrust to* [*paratíthēmi*] faithful men who will

---

7 Bernard Orchard, *A Catholic Commentary on Holy Scripture* (Nelson, 1953), 1147–1148.

be able to teach others also" (2 Tim. 2:2). Timothy is to entrust or deposit what he has heard from Paul to others.

There is an oral dimension to the *paratheken*. Paul tells Timothy, "But as for you, continue in what you have learned and have firmly believed, knowing from whom you learned it and how from childhood you have been acquainted with the sacred writings which are able to instruct you for salvation through faith in Christ Jesus" (2 Tim. 3:14–15). The deposit that Timothy received came to him orally and in written form. In Paul's letter to the Thessalonians, he writes, "So then, brethren, stand firm and hold to the traditions which you were taught by us, *either by word of mouth or by letter*" (2 Thess. 2:15, emphasis added).

When the scope is extended to the entire New Testament, the Greek verb *paratithemi* occurs "19 times, usually in the literal sense of 'laying' food before someone (Mark 6:41), or 'expounding' teaching (Acts 17:3)."[8] This canonical context implies that the *paratheken* or deposit given to Timothy has the ability to feed and nourish the faithful.

How did the Church Fathers and early Christian writers interpret 1 Timothy 6:20 in relation to the *paratheken*? The question is worthwhile because the

---

8   Geoffrey William Kittel and Gerhard Friedrich Bromiley, *Theological Dictionary of the New Testament* (Grand Rapids, MI: W. B. Eerdmans, 1985), 1180.

Church Fathers—extraordinary, ancient, recognized teachers of the faith through documentation and lived experience—are timely witnesses to the Tradition.[9] Hippolytus, a presbyter of the Church of Rome, possible disciple of St. Irenaeus, and "the most important theologian and the most prolific religious writer of the Roman Church in the pre-Constantinian era,"[10],[11] interprets the *paratheken* or "deposit" as revelations of God largely taken from Sacred Scripture.[12] Tertullian, one of the most important and original ecclesiastical authors in Latin,[13] sees the "deposit" as doctrine from Christ Jesus.[14] John Cassian (AD 360–435), monk and ascetic writer of southern Gaul,[15] understands the "deposit" to be the Sacred Scripture and morality.[16] Saint Vincent of

---

9   cf. Libreria Editrice Vaticana, *Catechism of the Catholic Church* (United States Conference of Catholic Bishops, 2011), 688.

10   J. P. Kirsch, "Hippolytus of Rome, Saint," *Catholic Encyclopedia*, The Faith Database CD-Rom (Third Millennium Media, 2008).

11   cf. Johannes Quasten, *Patrology. Volume 2: The Ante-Nicene Literature After Irenaeus. Volume 2 Only* (Newman Press, 1953).

12   Hippolytus, "The AntiChrist," *The Faith Database*, CD-ROM (Third Millennium Media, 2008).

13   Quasten, *Patrology. Volume 2.*

14   Tertullian, "The Prescription Against Heretics," *The Faith Database*, CD-ROM (Third Millennium Media, 2008).

15   Maurice Hassett, "John Cassian," *Catholic Encyclopedia*, The Faith Database CD-ROM (Third Millennium Media, 2008).

16   John Cassian, "Conference 14," *The Faith Database*, CD-ROM (Third Millennium Media, 2008).

Lerins, fifth-century priest and writer,[17] identifies the deposit with the rule of faith that has been passed down.[18] Vincent of Lerins writes:

> What is "The deposit"? That which has been entrusted to thee, not that which thou hast thyself devised: a matter not of wit, but of learning; not of private adoption, but of public tradition; a matter brought to thee, not put forth by thee, wherein thou art bound to be not an author but a keeper, not a teacher but a disciple, not a leader but a follower. "Keep the deposit." Preserve the talent of Catholic Faith inviolate, unadulterate. That which has been entrusted to thee, let it continue in thy possession, let it be handed on by thee. Thou hast received gold; give gold in turn. Do not substitute one thing for another. Do not for gold impudently substitute lead or brass. Give real gold, not counterfeit.[19]

The "deposit" is described as the Catholic faith that has been received and passed down—hence the term

---

17 Angelo [ed.]; Quasten, Johannes [intro.] di Berardino, *Patrology. Volume IV. The Golden Age of Latin Patristic Literature from the Council of Nicea to the Council of Chalcedon*, Reprint (Christian Classic Inc., 1991).

18 Vincent of Lerins, "Commonitory for the Antiquity and Universality of the Catholic Faith," *The Faith Database*, CD-ROM (Third Millennium Media, 2008).

19 Ibid.

"public tradition." This reality is precious as gold. The early Christian writers primarily interpreted the *paratheken* as being divinely revealed doctrines.

The writings of early Christians show a familiarity with the idea of deposit in relation to the Christian faith. St. Irenaeus (AD 120–180), bishop of Lyons and Father of the Church, writes the following: "The truth is to be found nowhere else but in the Catholic Church, the sole *depository* of apostolic doctrine. Heresies are of recent formation, and cannot trace their origin up to the apostles."[20] This "depository" is made up of teachings that found their origins in the apostles. The apostolic doctrines are the "truth" and are found in the Catholic Church. The apostles "lodged in her [the Church's] hands most copiously all things pertaining to the truth: so that every man, whosoever will, can draw from her the water of life."[21] Irenaeus also refers to the deposit as a "tradition of the truth" that is passed down orally and in written form.[22] As these apostolic doctrines are received, they become known as "the faith." Irenaeus writes, "[N]amely, our *faith*; which, having been received from the Church, we do preserve, and which always, by the Spirit of God, renew-

---

20 St. Irenaeus of Lyons, "Adversus Haereses (Book III, Chapter 4)," *The Faith Database*, CD-ROM (Third Millennium Media, 2008), Book III, Chapter 4.
21 St. Irenaeus of Lyons, "Adversus Haereses (Book III, Chapter 4)."
22 Ibid.

ing its youth, as if it were some precious *deposit* in an excellent vessel, causes the vessel itself containing it to renew its youth also."[23] This last quote is the rudimentary formation of the future phrase "deposit of faith."

Tertullian (AD 160–240) affirms this idea that the Catholic Church is a holding place of apostolic teaching: "Christ first delivered the faith. The apostles spread it; they founded churches as the *depositories* thereof. That faith, therefore, is apostolic, which descended from the apostles, through apostolic churches."[24] Tertullian also describes this apostolic doctrine as a "rule":

All doctrine true which comes through the Church from the apostles, who were taught by God through Christ. All opinion which has no such divine origin and apostolic tradition to show, is ipso facto false...From this, therefore, do we draw up our rule. Since the Lord Jesus Christ sent the apostles to preach, (our rule is) that no others ought to be received as preachers than those whom Christ appointed.[25]

---

23 St. Irenaeus of Lyons, "Adversus Haereses (Book III, Chapter 24)," *The Faith Database*, CD-ROM (Third Millennium Media, 2008), Book III, Chapter 24.

24 Tertullian, "The Prescription Against Heretics."

25 Ibid.

This rule is nothing less than what Christ has revealed through the apostolic preaching and writing.[26] Tertullian uses the phrase "rule of faith" in the same context as "deposit": "That comes down from the apostles, which has been kept as a sacred *deposit* in the churches of the apostles. Let us see what milk the Corinthians drank from Paul; to what *rule of faith* the Galatians were brought for correction."[27] The rule of faith is also identified as "fixed tenets" used to guide one's reading of Scripture or "records of faith."[28]

Basil the Great (AD 329–379), a bishop and Doctor of the Church, employs the term "deposit" in connection with apostolic teaching: "without suffering a wound in your faith, and as having kept the deposit of the apostles inviolate."[29] He contrasts this deposit of the apostles with "heretical impurity."[30] In Letter 105, St. Basil identifies the deposit with the central article of faith: "You have not abandoned the apostolic proclamation of faith…You have professed your faith in Father, Son and Holy Ghost. Do not

---

26 Ibid.

27 Tertullian, "Against Marcion, Book IV," *The Faith Database*, CD-ROM (Third Millennium Media, 2008). (emphasis in the original text)

28 cf. Tertullian, "The Prescription Against Heretics."

29 St. Basil the Great, "Letter 242," *The Faith Database*, CD-ROM (Third Millennium Media, 2008).

30 Ibid.

abandon this deposit."[31] Basil identifies the deposit with the doctrine of the Trinity.

St. Gregory of Nyssa (AD 325–386), one of the Cappadocian Fathers, explicitly uses the phrase "deposit of faith." He writes, "Would it not have been safer for all, following the counsel of wisdom, to abstain from searching into such deep matters, and in peace and quietness to keep inviolate the pure deposit of the faith?"[32] He goes on to speak of the contents of this deposit:

> Yet perchance they would have done better to look to the sacred company of the Prophets and Patriarchs, to whom "at sundry times, and in divers manners(6)," the Word of truth spake, and, next in order, those who were eye-witnesses and ministers of the word, that they might give honour due to the claims on their belief of the things attested by the Holy Spirit Himself, and abide within the limits of their teaching and knowledge, and not venture on themes which are not comprehended in the canon of the sacred writers.[33]

---

31 St. Basil the Great, "Letter 105," *The Faith Database*, CD-ROM (Third Millennium Media, 2008).

32 St. Gregory of Nyssa, "Answer to Eunomius' Second Book," *The Faith Database*, CD-ROM (Third Millennium Media, 2008).

33 Ibid.

The "Prophets and Patriarchs" seems to be a reference to the Old Testament. "Eye-witnesses and ministers of the word" appears to be a reference to the Gospel accounts and the New Testament in general. The reader is encouraged not to wander into "themes" not understood in the Sacred Scripture. The use of "themes" implicitly suggests that all subject matters of the deposit can be found in the Scriptures. Again, the deposit is used as a reference to divine teaching.

St. Cyril of Jerusalem, bishop and doctor of the Church, identifies the deposit with articles of faith contained in the creeds, which can be confirmed in the Sacred Scriptures. These articles of faith are a Tradition. He writes:

> So for the present listen while I simply say the Creed, and commit it to memory; but at the proper season expect the confirmation out of Holy Scripture of each part of the contents. For the articles of the Faith were not composed as seemed good to men; but the most important points collected out of all the Scripture make up one complete teaching of the Faith. And just as the mustard seed in one small grain contains many branches, so also this Faith has embraced in few words all the knowledge of godliness in the Old and New

Testaments. Take heed then, brethren, and hold fast the traditions which ye now receive, and write them on the table of your heart.[34]

He goes on to describe these articles of faith as a kind of deposit:

Guard them with reverence, lest per chance the enemy despoil any who have grown slack; or lest some heretic pervert any of the truths delivered to you. For faith is like putting money into the bank, even as we have now done; but from you God requires the accounts of the deposit. I charge you, as the Apostle saith, before God, who quickeneth all things, and Christ Jesus, who before Pontius Pilate witnessed the good confession, that ye keep this faith which is committed to you, without spot, until the appearing of our Lord Jesus Christ. A treasure of life has now been committed to thee...[35]

As St. Basil the Great relates the deposit with a specific article of the Faith, St. Cyril of Jerusalem follows suit. In another of Cyril's lectures, he writes:

---

34   St. Cyril of Jerusalem, "Catechetical Lecture 5," *The Faith Database*, CD-ROM (Third Millennium Media, 2008).

35   Ibid.

Was it without reason that Christ was made Man? Are our teachings ingenious phrases and human subtleties? Are not the Holy Scriptures our salvation? Are not the predictions of the Prophets? Keep then, I pray thee, this deposit undisturbed, and let none remove thee: believe that God became Man.[36]

Cyril uses the term "deposit" to label the second most central doctrine in Christianity: the Incarnation. The Incarnation is divine revelation given for the sake of salvation, which is nothing less than being a partaker of the divine life. This deposit is given not for mere intellectual entertainment but for the intention of meeting God! God takes on human nature so that human nature can be divinized.

For St. Gregory of Nazianzen, another Cappadocian Father, the deposit is marked with the teaching of the Trinity as seen earlier with St. Basil. He writes, "Besides all this and before all, keep I pray you the good deposit, by which I live and work, and which I desire to have as the companion of my departure; with which I endure all that is so distressful, and despise all delights; the confession of the Father and the Son and the Holy Ghost."[37]

---

36 St. Cyril of Jerusalem, "Catechetical Lecture 12," *The Faith Database*, CD-ROM (Third Millennium Media, 2008).

37 St. Gregory Nazianzen, "Oration 40," *The Faith Database*, CD-ROM (Third Millennium Media, 2008).

John Chrysostom (AD 347–407), another Doctor of the Church, employs the term "deposit" in a variety of contexts. He describes the profession of faith, in particular the denouncing of Satan, as a deposit. He writes:

> If thou wilt remember that word, which thou sentest forth when thou wert initiated, I renounce thee, Satan, and thy pomp, and thy service...Let us then say this, "I renounce thee, Satan," as men who are about in that world at that day to have that word demanded of them, and let us keep it in order that we may then return this deposit safe.[38]

Chrysostom also identifies the deposit with words of the apostles: "For what can the pearl of a king do like that which the words of an Apostle effected?...I deposit the treasure."[39] In his homily on Acts of the Apostles, Chrysostom describes the testimony of the apostles about Resurrection as a deposit: "And with great power the Apostles rendered their testimony (apedidoun) of the resurrection. The phrase betokens them to be as persons put in trust with a

---

38 St. John Chrysostom, "Instructions to Catechumans," *The Faith Database*, CD-ROM (Third Millennium Media, 2008).

39 St. John Chrysostom, "Second Homily on Eutropius (After His Captivity)," *The Faith Database*, CD-ROM (Third Millennium Media, 2008).

deposit..."[40] Chrysostom, in a commentary on 1 Corinthians 15:1, designates the Gospel as a deposit:

> Seest thou how he calls themselves to be witnesses of the things spoken? And he saith not, "which ye heard," but, "which ye received," demanding it of them as a kind of deposit, and showing that not in word only, but also by deeds and signs and wonders they received it, and that they should hold it safe.[41]

An interesting item to note is that in this example, the "deposit" is not just words but deeds, signs, and wonders. In his commentary on 1 Timothy, he describes deposit or trust as being equivalent to the belief of the Incarnation: "...Great is the mystery...For God became Man...In keeping this mystery, then, let us be faithful to our trust."[42] Chrysostom also uses "deposit" to reference actions or morality:

> Now the usury of hearing is the manifestation of it by deeds, for the deposit is the Lord's.

---

40 St. John Chrysostom, "Homily 11 on the Acts of the Apostles ACTS IV. 23," *The Faith Database*, CD-ROM (Third Millennium Media, 2008).

41 St. John Chrysostom, "Homily 38 on First Corinthians," *The Faith Database*, CD-ROM (Third Millennium Media, 2008).

42 St. John Chrysostom, "Homily 11 on First Timothy," *The Faith Database*, CD-ROM (Third Millennium Media, 2008).

Therefore let us not negligently receive that with which we are entrusted. But let us keep it with diligence, that we may restore it with much interest on That Day. For unless thou bring others to the performance of the same good works, thou shalt hear that voice, which he who buried the talent heard.[43]

Pope Leo the Great (AD 395–461) uses the term "deposit" in a sermon dedicated to the martyrdom of St. Lawrence. He writes:

The description of his sufferings continued. The baffled plunderer, therefore, frets, and blazing out into hatred of a religion, which had put riches to such a use, determines to pillage a still greater treasure by carrying off that sacred deposit, wherewith he was enriched, as he could find no solid hoard of money in his possession. He orders Laurentius to renounce Christ.[44]

The deposit, in this case, is faith in Christ, which is a result of Christ's love.[45] Leo the Great also uses "de-

---

43 St. John Chrysostom, "Homily 12 on the Statues," *The Faith Database*, CD-ROM (Third Millennium Media, 2008).

44 St. Leo the Great, "Sermon 85," *The Faith Database*, CD-ROM (Third Millennium Media, 2008).

45 Ibid.

posit" to label a body of knowledge: "He therefore who had spoken to Moses, spoke also to the apostles, and the swift hand of the Word wrote and deposited the secrets of the new covenant in the disciples' hearts."[46]

What has one learned after this survey of the Scriptures and early ecclesiastical writers on the concept of the deposit of faith? For starters, the phrase "deposit of faith" is definitely at its infancy stage. The reality of a deposit is well attested though. The Sacred Scriptures portray the deposit as primarily revealed teachings or doctrines by Christ and the Holy Spirit that have been entrusted to the apostles. These teachings are not mere words or ordinances but have a salvific and nourishing instrumentality. The words of Christ are the words of God that must be safeguarded as a treasure. These doctrines extend beyond what is to be believed and are also concerned with what is to be done. Faith and morals are both at stake. This deposit of Christ is passed down in the life of the Church in both written and oral formats. The early Church writers would, at times, identify the deposit with a particular article of faith or with the entire Gospel message. Another phrase used to describe the reality of the deposit is "rule

---

46 St. Leo the Great, "Sermon 95," *The Faith Database*, CD-ROM (Third Millennium Media, 2008).

of faith" or simply "the faith." The Fathers placed great emphasis on the fact that the deposit is apostolic teaching, which has often been summarized in creeds (professions of faith).

CHAPTER 2

Magisterial Precedence to Vatican II (Trent/Vatican I)

—⟋ɯ⟍—

THIS CHAPTER WILL EXPLORE HOW the Church has used the phrase "deposit of faith" or "deposit" after the Patristic era and prior to the beginning of the Second Vatican Council, which began in 1962. As stated in chapter 1, the use of the term "deposit" can be traced back to Sacred Scriptures. It can be seen in the early history of the Church. The term "deposit" is not, however, in use in the Middle Ages.[1] A resurgence of the term occurs in the eighteenth century, which is precisely the time period marked for the age of the Enlightenment. The period of the Enlightenment is known for the exaltation of empiricism and rational thought to the exclusion of divine revelation and dogma. The Church has always responded to the errors of the time in order to better

---

1 P. F. Chirico, "Deposit of Faith," *New Catholic Encyclopedia* (Gale Group in association with the Catholic University of America, 2003), Vol. 14, 675.

advance the Kingdom and serve the faithful in their spiritual lives. Several encyclicals and ecumenical councils will be examined for the use of the term "deposit" or the phrase "deposit of faith."

The first ecumenical council to use the term "deposit" in reference to Christ's Revelation was the Council of Trent. During the fourth session in the "Decree of Reception of the Sacred Books and Apostolic Traditions," the council fathers state, "The Council clearly perceives that this truth and rule are contained in the written books and unwritten traditions which have come down to us..."[2] The phrase "this truth" is a reference to truth of Christ, which is also identified as "the deposit."[3] The historical background to the Council of Trent was the Protestant Reformation, which set forth the doctrine of Sola Scriptura. The Bible alone was the sole infallible rule of faith for the reformers. The Council of Trent definitively responded to this false doctrine.

In 1766, Pope Clement XIII promulgates an encyclical to his fellow bishops on the dangers of anti-Christian writings. He writes, "It is principally your duty to stand as a wall so that no foundation can be

---

2 Jacques Dupuis, *The Christian Faith: In the Doctrinal Documents of the Catholic Church*, 7th Rev. (Alba House, 2001).

3 Addis and Arnold, "Deposit of Faith," in *Catholic Dictionary: Containing Some Account of the Doctrine, Discipline, Rites, Ceremonies, Councils, and Religious Orders of the Catholic Church*, 9th ed. (St. Louis, MO.: B. Herder, 1917), 876.

laid other than the one that is already laid. Watch over the most holy deposit of faith to whose protection you committed yourselves on oath at your solemn consecration."[4] The context reveals that the deposit of faith being referred to here is the truths of the Catholic faith, religion, and good morals.[5]

In 1769, Pope Clement uses the phrase "deposit of faith" in his encyclical "Proclaiming a Universal Jubilee." He writes:

> By His own laws and institutions He founded and reinforced this holy city which is His Church. To it he entrusted, as it were, the deposit of faith in Him to be preserved piously and without contamination. He wished it to be the bulwark of His teaching and truth against which the gates of hell would never prevail. We, therefore, the overseers and guardians of this holy city, must preserve the magnificent heritage of Our laws and faith which has been passed down intact to Us.[6]

The Church has the responsibility of guarding Jesus's teachings and truth. The deposit of faith is

---

4 Pope Clement XIII, "On the Dangers of Anti-Christian Writings," *The Faith Database*, CD-ROM (Third Millennium Media, 2008).

5 cf. Ibid.

6 Pope Clement XIV, "Proclaiming a Universal Jubilee," *The Faith Database*, CD-ROM (Third Millennium Media, 2008).

sound doctrine as well as the Word of God found in the Sacred Scripture and in the "footsteps of our ancestors" or tradition.[7] This deposit is a "heritage of laws and faith."[8]

In 1775, Pope Pius VI promulgates an encyclical that also uses "the deposit": "These are the chief matters on which We wanted to address you in the Lord, Venerable Brothers. We urgently ask that We may personally experience the pleasure of us all harmoniously preserving faithfully the deposit entrusted to Our keeping."[9] What are "the chief matters"? The chief matters are erroneous doctrines that are dangerous to the salvation of souls. These doctrines need to be battled with the purity of the Catholic faith and truth. He writes, "Since it concerns the entire body of the Church, it is a special concern of yours because you are called to share in Our pastoral concern, and the purity of the faith is particularly entrusted to your watchfulness."[10] The "deposit" is a reference to the Catholic faith, truth, Sacred Scripture, and the Gospel. The pope clearly has an urgent tone for the protection of this deposit, which ultimately leads to a personal encounter with Christ: salvation. Salvation is not only from sin but

---

7   cf. Ibid.

8   cf. Ibid.

9   Pope Pius VI, "Problems of the Pontificate," *The Faith Database*, CD-ROM (Third Millennium Media, 2008).

10   Ibid.

for an abundant life in Christ, and the bishops have the duty of protecting the deposit that leads to that supernatural life.

The nineteenth century continues this pattern of using "deposit" to refer to sound, God-given doctrine. In 1800, Pope Pius VII wrote, "Therefore, omit no watchfulness, diligence, care, and effort, in order to 'guard the deposit' of Christ's teaching whose destruction has been planned, as you know, by a great conspiracy."[11] "The deposit" is used to address the teaching of Christ.

Pope Gregory XVI, in 1833, uses the phrase "deposit of faith" in the context of sacred doctrine and the Catholic religion.[12] "The Catholic religion" seems to open the phrase "deposit of faith" to more than just sacred doctrine. He also uses the phrase to indicate "supernatural truths."[13]

In 1854 Pope Pius IX writes in his Papal Bull that defined the Immaculate Conception, "The Catholic Church, directed by the Holy Spirit of God, is the pillar and base of truth and has ever held as divinely revealed and as contained in the deposit of heavenly

---

11 Pope Pius VII, "Return to Gospel Principles," *The Faith Database*, CD-ROM (Third Millennium Media, 2008).

12 cf. Pope Gregory XVI, "On the 'Pragmatic Constitution,'" *The Faith Database*, CD-ROM (Third Millennium Media, 2008).

13 cf. Pope Gregory XVI, "Condemnation of the Works of George Hermes," ed. Denzinger, *Welcome to the Catholic Church*, CD-ROM (Harmony Media, 2007).

revelation this doctrine concerning the original innocence of the august Virgin..."[14] "The deposit," again, is referring to God's revealed doctrine. In his letter "The False Freedom of Science," Pius IX gives a salvific instrumentality to the deposit of faith:

> For the Church, from her divine institution, has the duty both to hold most diligently to the deposit of faith, whole and inviolate, and to watch continually with great earnestness over the salvation of souls, and with the greatest care to remove and eliminate all those things which can be opposed to faith or can in any way endanger the salvation of souls.[15]

The term "deposit of faith" came into prominent use at the First Vatican Council (1869–1870).[16] This council saw the promulgations of two dogmatic constitutions: "Dogmatic Constitution on the Catholic Faith" and "The Dogmatic Constitution on the Church of Christ." Vatican I was the Church's response to the growing

---

14   Pope Pius IX, "Ineffabilis Deus," *Welcome to the Catholic Church*, CD-ROM (Harmony Media, 2007).

15   Pius IX, "The False Freedom of Science (against James Frohschammer)," ed. Denzinger, *Welcome to the Catholic Church*, CD-ROM (Harmony Media, 2007).

16   cf. Nicholas Rademacher, "Deposit of Faith," ed. Glazier and Hellwig, *The Modern Catholic Encyclopedia* (Collegeville, Minn: Liturgical Press, c2004).

trend of "pantheism, materialism and atheism."[17] The "Dogmatic Constitution on the Catholic Faith" is divided into four chapters, and the "deposit" is used twice in chapter 4, which is entitled "Faith and Reason." Chapter 4 begins with a discussion on the twofold order of knowledge: faith and reason. The two are never in disagreement because they both have one source: God Himself. The chapter goes on to present the Church's ability and duty to judge the world's philosophies while protecting her "deposit of faith."

The council states:

> Further, the Church which, together with the apostolic duty of teaching, has received the command to guard the deposit of faith, has also, from divine Providence, the right and duty of proscribing "knowledge falsely so called" [1 Tim. 6:20], "lest anyone be cheated by philosophy and vain deceit" [cf. Col. 2:8; can. 2]. Wherefore, all faithful Christians not only are forbidden to defend opinions of this sort, which are known to be contrary to the teaching of faith, especially if they have been condemned by the Church, as the legitimate conclusions of science, but they shall be altogether bound to hold them rather as

---

17 Vatican I, "Dogmatic Constitution on the Catholic Faith," *The Faith Database*, CD-ROM (Third Millennium Media, 2008).

errors, which present a false appearance of truth.[18]

This "deposit of faith" is the teaching or doctrine passed from Christ to His Church. This body of sacred knowledge is received, not created. Therefore, this knowledge can never be reduced or increased. The "deposit" should never be looked at as another kind of philosophy:

> For, the doctrine of faith which God revealed has not been handed down as a philosophic invention to the human mind to be perfected, but has been entrusted as a divine deposit to the Spouse of Christ, to be faithfully guarded and infallibly interpreted. Hence, also, that understanding of its sacred dogmas must be perpetually retained, which Holy Mother Church has once declared; and there must never be recession from that meaning under the specious name of a deeper understanding [can. 3]. "Therefore...let the understanding, the knowledge, and wisdom of individuals as of all, of one man as of the whole Church, grow and progress strongly with the passage of the ages and the centuries; but let it be

18   Vatican I, "Dogmatic Constitution Concerning the Catholic Faith (1798)," ed. Denzinger, *Welcome to the Catholic Church*, CD-ROM (Harmony Media, 2007), 1798.

solely in its own genus, namely in the same dogma, with the same sense and the same understanding.[19]

The content of the "deposit" is static. This understanding was being challenged by the rise of historical consciousness and ideas grounded in evolutionary biology, which tended to undercut the timeless truths of God's revelation.[20] There is development of doctrine that is different and is a reflection of the faithful's understanding of the deposit constantly growing.

The "Dogmatic Constitution on the Church of Christ," which definitively set forth Papal Infallibility, uses the term "deposit of faith" once. The council writes:

For, the Holy Spirit was not promised to the successors of Peter that by His revelation they might disclose new doctrine, but that by His help they might guard sacredly the revelation transmitted through the apostles and the deposit of faith, and might faithfully set it forth. Indeed, all the venerable fathers have embraced their apostolic doctrine, and the holy orthodox Doctors have venerated and followed it, knowing full well that the

---

19   Vatican I, "Dogmatic Constitution Concerning the Catholic Faith (1800)," ed. Denzinger, *Welcome to the Catholic Church*, CD-ROM (Harmony Media, 2007).

20   cf. Nicholas Rademacher, "Deposit of Faith."

> See of St. Peter always remains unimpaired
> by any error, according to the divine promise
> of our Lord the Savior made to the chief of
> His disciples: "I have prayed for thee, that thy
> faith fail not: and thou, being once converted,
> confirm thy brethren" (Luke 22:32).[21]

The sentence before this quote reveals the sources of divine revelation and contents of the deposit of faith: Scripture and Apostolic Tradition. The charism of Papal Infallibility is closely tied to the protection and guarding of the deposit of faith. Papal Infallibility is a gift from Jesus and the Holy Spirit to protect the divine doctrine, which must be preserved. The deposit is concerned with supernatural truth: "The truths revealed or spoken by God are contained in the holy books and in tradition. They constitute revelation...entrusted to the Church by Christ as a deposit to be...protected against error."[22]

Pope Leo XIII, in 1897, uses the term "deposit" in his encyclical on the Holy Spirit: "Thus was fully accomplished that last promise of Christ to His apostles of sending the Holy Ghost, who was to complete and,

---

21   Vatican I, "Dogmatic Constitution on the Church of Christ (1836)," ed. Denzinger, *Welcome to the Catholic Church*, CD-ROM (Harmony Media, 2007).

22   Latourelle, *Theology of Revelation: Including a Commentary on the Constitution "Dei Verbum" of Vatican II* (Staten Island, NY: Alba House, 1966), 266.

as it were, to seal the deposit of doctrine committed to them under His inspiration."[23] Again, revealed doctrine or truth committed to the apostles under the inspiration of the Holy Spirit is referenced.

In 1907, Pope Pius X uses "deposit of faith" in his letter on the doctrine of the Modernists:

> One of the primary obligations assigned by Christ to the office divinely committed to Us of feeding the Lord's flock is that of guarding with the greatest vigilance the deposit of the faith delivered to the saints, rejecting the profane novelties of words and the gainsaying of knowledge falsely so called.[24]

The phrase "deposit of faith" indicates true sacred knowledge that feeds the faithful. The text "delivered to the saints" brings to mind Jude 3. Biblical commentary states that "faith" is *fides quae creditur*, a body of doctrine. The word "deliver," "hand on" (*paradidōmi*), is a quasi-technical term in the New Testament for the handing down of teachings received in the community."[25] Pius's encyclical on St.

---

23 Pope Leo XIII, "Divinum Illud Munus," *Welcome to the Catholic Church*, CD-ROM (Harmony Media, 2007), #5.

24 Pope Pius X, "Pascendi Dominici Gregis," *Welcome to the Catholic Church*, CD-ROM (Harmony Media, 2007), #1.

25 Roland Edmund Brown, Raymond Edward, and Joseph A. Fitzmyer, *The Jerome Biblical Commentary* (Englewood Cliffs, NJ: Prentice-Hall, 1996), Jud 3.

Charles Borromeo describes the deposit in the context of "saving waters of truth and life," which has two aspects: doctrines and morality.[26]

In 1928, Pope Pius XI writes an encyclical on religious unity. He uses the phrases "deposit of truth" and "deposit of Revelation."[27] Given the context, the following items are being referenced: God's Word through the prophets and Jesus, doctrines of faith and morals, revealed doctrines, and articles of faith.[28] The moral truth given by God is identified with Pius XI's usage of "deposit" in his encyclical "On the Reconstruction of the Social Order": "[B]ut in all things that are connected with the moral law. For as to these, the deposit of truth that God committed to Us and the grave duty of disseminating and interpreting the whole moral law."[29] The deposit seems to be branded as things connected with the moral law and closely connected to the duty to spread and interpret the moral law.

In 1947, Pope Pius XII writes an encyclical on the liturgy. He employs the term "deposit of faith" in it.[30]

---

26 cf. Pope Pius X, "Editae Saepe," *Welcome to the Catholic Church*, CD-ROM (Harmony Media, 2007), #29.

27 cf. Pope Pius XI, "Mortalium Animos," *Welcome to the Catholic Church*, CD-ROM (Harmony Media, 2007), #8.

28 cf. Ibid.

29 Pope Pius XI, "Quadragesimo Anno," *Welcome to the Catholic Church*, CD-ROM (Harmony Media, 2007), #41.

30 cf. Pope Pius XII, "Mediator Dei (on the Sacred Liturgy)," *The Faith Database*, CD-ROM (Third Millennium Media, 2008), #64.

This example seems to expand the use of "deposit" to matters of worship also.

Pope Pius XII uses the term "deposit" six different times in his encyclical "Humani Generis" in 1950. He writes:

> And although this sacred Office of Teacher in matters of faith and morals must be the proximate and universal criterion of truth for all theologians, since to it has been entrusted by Christ Our Lord the whole deposit of faith—Sacred Scripture and divine Tradition—to be preserved, guarded and interpreted...[31]

The sources of revelation, Sacred Scripture, and Sacred Tradition are the contents of the "whole deposit of faith." Pius XII goes on to write:

> For, together with the sources of positive theology God has given to His Church a living Teaching Authority to elucidate and explain what is contained in the deposit of faith only obscurely and implicitly. This deposit of faith our Divine Redeemer has given for authentic interpretation not to each of the faithful.[32]

---

31 Pope Pius XII, "Humani Generis," *Welcome to the Catholic Church*, CD-ROM (Harmony Media, 2007), #18.

32 Ibid., #21.

Divine teaching continues to be the primary meaning behind the "deposit of faith." The deposit is a divine treasure trove that theology dives deeper into. This treasure will never be exhausted. Pius XII writes, "Hence it is that theology through the study of its sacred sources remains ever fresh; on the other hand, speculation which neglects a deeper search into the deposit of faith, proves sterile, as we know from experience."[33] The other three uses of "deposit" are consistent with the others. "Catholic dogma" is another term Pope Pius XII employs in discussing the deposit, which confirms the primary meaning of deposit of faith as being divinely revealed teaching.

The year 1950 is well known for being the year that Pope Pius XII officially promulgated the dogma of the Assumption of Mary. In this declaration, the term "deposit" is used. He writes:

> Those whom "the Holy Ghost has placed as bishops to rule the Church of God" gave an almost unanimous affirmative response to both these questions. This "outstanding agreement of the Catholic prelates and the faithful," affirming that the bodily Assumption of God's Mother into heaven can be defined as a dogma of faith, since it shows us the concordant

---

33 Ibid.

teaching of the Church's ordinary doctrinal authority and the concordant faith of the Christian people, which the same doctrinal authority sustains and directs, thus by itself, and in an entirely certain and infallible way, manifested this privilege as a truth revealed by God and contained in that divine deposit which Christ has delivered to His Spouse to be guarded faithfully and to be taught infallibly.[34]

The Assumption of Mary is part of the deposit of faith, meaning it is a revealed truth.

In 1961, Pope John XXIII wrote the document "Message of Peace." He writes, "Possessing the wisdom and the fullness of fatherhood as the humble successor of St. Peter and custodian of the Deposit of Faith—which remains always the great Divine Book open to all men of all nations—and consequently also the keeper of Christ's Gospel."[35] In this quote, the deposit of faith is identified with the written source of revelation, which is Sacred Scripture.

The magisterial usage of the term "deposit" or "deposit of faith" is very consistent. The deposit of faith is the Word of God or divine teaching from

---

34 Pope Pius XII, "Munificentissimus Deus," *Welcome to the Catholic Church*, CD-ROM (Harmony Media, 2007), Section II.

35 Pope John XXIII, "Message of Peace," *Welcome to the Catholic Church*, CD-ROM (Harmony Media, 2007), intro.

Jesus that the Holy Spirit transmitted to the apostles and passed down to the Church. It is now protected by the Spirit-led Magisterium, the successors of the apostles. This apostolic teaching deals with articles of faith as well as morals. Oral and written are the two forms in which the deposit is given to the Church. This doctrine is not merely abstract intellectual truths but also a reality that is destined to bring the faithful into a living knowledge of the Lord, which is eternal life (cf. John 17:3). The deposit of faith has a salvific instrumentality. It enables the faithful to have access to supernatural truths that are inaccessible to human nature in and of itself. The use of the term "deposit of faith" in reference to the Gospel and the Catholic religion implies a connection not only with divine teaching but with divine presence and power as well. Matters of the liturgy are also included.

CHAPTER 3

Vatican II's Expression

—⁓—

THIS CHAPTER WILL EXPLORE THE deposit of faith as expressed in the Second Vatican Council. Vatican II is the most recent ecumenical council and is critical to any discussion on the essence of the deposit of faith. Even though it was primarily a pastoral council, seeing that no new definitive teaching arose as a result, the meeting still affirms infallible teachings that have been passed down in the life of the Church. In the sixteen documents of the council, the term "deposit" was used seven times. *Lumen Gentium* uses the phrases "deposit of Revelation" and "deposit of faith" (LG 25). *Gaudium et Spes* and *Unitatis Redintegratio* use the phrase "deposit of faith" also (GS 62, UR 6). *Dei Verbum* uses "deposit of the word of God," "deposit," and "deposit of faith" (DV 10). Given that *Dei Verbum* is the "Dogmatic Constitution on Divine Revelation," it makes sense to first deal with how this document treats the deposit of faith. As a result, other references to the deposit of faith from other documents will be interpreted through the lens of *Dei Verbum.*

Dei Verbum is divided into seven sections. The second section deals with the essence of revelation itself. The definition of revelation does not get bogged down into the age-old controversy of the "two-source" theory but appeals to a more personal and integrative understanding of the essence of revelation.[1] *Dei Verbum* leaves open the question of material sufficiency of Scripture but does something much needed in the discussion of divine revelation. Divine revelation is identified with God Himself and His will for us (DV 2). This revelation is realized in the world through God's activity and speech (DV 2). God's deeds and words have an inner unity and shed light on one another (DV 2). According to Cardinal Ratzinger, the emphasis on "deeds and words" helps to avoid revelation being reduced to supernatural truths known through an assenting reason.[2] Revelation is ultimately a Person! Jesus is the mediator and fullness of all revelation (DV 2). Jesus speaks the words of God and completes the work of salvation (DV 4). Eric de Moulins-Beaufort, a priest in the diocese of Paris, states:

---

1   cf. "Dogmatic Constitution on Divine Revelation," ed. Herbert Vorgrimler, *Commentary on the Documents of Vatican II* (New York: Crossroad, 1989), 170; 182.

2   cf. Joseph Ratzinger, "Dogmatic Constitution on Divine Revelation."

The greatest contribution of *Dei Verbum*...is therefore that it no longer presents revelation as a communication of truths in the form of verbal locutions, but in accord with how revelation presents itself: as a free act of God, a personal act which is also God's opening up of his personal mystery.[3]

The term "deposit" does not surface until the third section of *Dei Verbum*, which is entitled "Handing on Divine Revelation." The purpose of the "deposit," even before its essence is discussed, has to be viewed as a means through which God Himself is communicated or handed on. Thomas Norris comments:

Since the rubric, "the word of God", is a synonym for divine revelation in *DV*, one may see here the concern of the Council Fathers to define Scripture and Tradition in a way that was more patristic, more catholic and more historical, and, by the same token, less polemical. In this perspective, Scripture, Tradition, and Magisterium are not primarily fonts of divine revelation but its media, its carriers.[4]

---

3 E. de Moulins-Beaufort, "Henri de Lubac : Reader of Dei Verbum," *Communion/International Catholic Review* 28, no. 4 (2001): 669–694.

4 T. Norris, "On Revisiting Dei Verbum," *Irish Theological Quarterly* 66, no. 4 (2001): 315–337.

Sacred Scripture and Sacred Tradition are the main components of the deposit of faith. These constituents form a necessary embodiment and expression of divine revelation.[5]

Divine revelation is handed on through Sacred Tradition and Sacred Scripture: "Sacred tradition and Sacred Scripture form one sacred deposit of the word of God, committed to the Church" (*DV* 10). The origin and essence of Tradition has been expanded when one compares Trent's formulations to *Dei Verbum*'s. *Dei Verbum* adds to Trent's formulation by adding *"adimplevit"* and *"eis sona divina communicantes."*[6] Ratzinger states:

> By describing the activity of Jesus in relation to the Gospel not only as "promulgating," but also as "fulfilling," it plays down the narrow legal aspect to which the categorization of the Christian message under the idea of *nova lex* had ultimately led, which is what lies behind the concept of promulgation.[7]

Dei Verbum makes it a point to show that what the apostles received and handed on was much more than mere teaching or law. Ratzinger continues to

---

5 cf. Ibid.

6 cf. Joseph Ratzinger, "Dogmatic Constitution on Divine Revelation."

7 Ibid.

point out how the Council of Trent identifies the origin of Tradition as Christ's and His apostles' preaching, whereas *Dei Verbum* identifies three different kinds of events: the Word of Lord, the apostles living with Him, and the apostles seeing what He did.[8] The apostles also passed down what they learned at the prompting of the Holy Spirit (DV 7). Ratzinger continues to describe the opening up of the character of Revelation:

> The point is certainly not to play off the theology of salvation history against word theology, but in the place of a narrowly doctrinal conception of revelation, as had been expressed in the Tridentine word theology, to open up a comprehensive view of the real character of revelation, which—precisely because it is concerned with the whole man—is founded not only in the word that Christ preached, but in the whole of the living experience of his person, thus embracing what is said and what is unsaid, what the Apostles in their turn are not able to express fully in words, but which is found in the whole reality of the Christian existence of which they speak, far transcending the framework of what has been explicitly formulated in words.[9]

---

8   Ibid., DV 7.
9   Ibid., 182.

This lived experience of the Lord is preserved in the Church. *Dei Verbum* states, "[S]o the Church, in her teaching, life and worship, perpetuates and hands on to all generations all that she herself is, all that she believes" (DV 8). The Tradition is nothing less than the Church's identity, Christ's bride that has become one flesh with her bridegroom (cf. Eph. 5:31–32). The Tradition is the "whole Christ," according to St. Augustine, being communicated or handed down to the faithful.

This rich and broad sense of the deposit of faith seems to be returning to the view found in Sacred Scripture, when the term "deposit" was used for more than dogmatic formulations. Yves M. J. Congar, in his commentary on *Tradition in the Old and New Testaments*, notes:

> An adequate theology of revelation shows that all its weight bears on the vital covenant relationship that God wants to establish with men…The collection of events, truths, and realities, which constitute or form the basis of this relationship between men and God in Christ, has been given once and for all by the apostles, and no one can substantially add to it.[10]

10 Yves Congar, *Tradition and Traditions: The Biblical, Historical, and Theological Evidence for Catholic Teaching on Tradition*, 2nd ed. (Ginn Pr, 1997), 21.

Brian J. Braman, SJ, has a very interesting and accurate way of describing the deposit of faith. He notes that *Dei Verbum* uses "deposit of faith" three times. He gives the following depiction of the deposit of faith:

Thus the deposit of faith is the incorporation of scripture, moral teachings, the sacramental life, and doctrinal life of the Church...Both Scripture and Tradition express this gift of God's self-giving-disclosure to his people. Through the gift of his Son and his Spirit, the Father is the living presence in the Body of Christ which is the Church. The Triune God invests his life in his people; he entrusts and discloses ("deposits") himself to them through the incarnation, life, death and resurrection of Christ, and the coming of the Holy Spirit...The deposit of the faith is not ours to do with as we please. It is the loving gift of the triune God who has "deposited" his life in us, transforming our minds and hearts with his beauty, truth, and love.[11]

He begins by identifying the deposit with Scripture and Tradition. Then he moves beyond this and sees Scripture and Tradition as expressers of God's

---

11   Brian J. Braman, "Opinion Polls and the Deposit of Faith," *Homiletic and Pastoral Review* 87 (November 1986): 65–69.

self-donation. The deposit is ultimately identified with the "gift of the triune God who has 'deposited' his life in us" through the life, death, and resurrection of Christ and the sending of the Holy Spirit.

Sacred Scripture and Sacred Tradition should not be seen as two separate sources. Revelation is a cohesive whole with one source: God.[12] As Hahnenberg states, "It is this cohesive whole that is passed on in different ways, both in writing and in the practices of the church."[13]

Sacred Scripture is explicitly described as the Word of God (*DV* 9). The Sacred Scripture is "God breathed" and therefore inspired. Sacred Scripture is presented as being distinct but also part of the larger category of Tradition. The teaching authority of the Church, the Magisterium, serves both Sacred Tradition and Sacred Scripture. All three realities are in need of one another in order for their preservation:

It is clear, therefore, that sacred tradition, Sacred Scripture and the teaching authority of the Church, in accord with God's most wise design, are so linked and joined together that one cannot stand without the others, and that all together and each in its own way under

---

12   cf. Hahnenberg, *Concise Guide To The Documents of Vatican II* (Cincinnati, Ohio: St. Anthony Messenger Press, c2007), 31.
13   Ibid.

the action of the one Holy Spirit contribute effectively to the salvation of souls (*DV* 10).

The Church draws from this rich deposit of faith whenever she teaches something for belief that is divinely revealed.

Dei Verbum has renewed and deepened the Church's understanding of the deposit of faith. The deposit does include dogmatic formulations, but this is just the surface of the rich reality of the deposit. The use of the term "surface" does not imply that dogma is somehow less important or disposable. It only suggests that there is so much more to the reality of the deposit of faith. This deposit has the duty of transmitting Jesus Himself, the essence and fullness of divine revelation. The dogmatic formulations are one part of the mirror (cf. *DV* 7) that reflects God. Jesus is not only the Truth but the Way and the Life as well (cf. John. 14:6). The "Way and Life" are also handed down to us through the deposit of faith, which goes beyond mere use of words and includes the preservation of God's intervening presence in salvation history, namely in Christ.

As mentioned earlier, *Lumen Gentium*, "The Dogmatic Constitution on the Church," uses the phrases "deposit of Revelation" and "deposit of faith" (*LG* 25). The chapter that they are used in is entitled "On the Hierarchical Structure of the Church and in Particular on the Episcopate." The first usage of "deposit" appears in the context of a discussion on papal infallibility. *Lumen Gentium* states:

> And this infallibility with which the Divine Redeemer willed His Church to be endowed in defining doctrine of faith and morals, extends as far as the deposit of Revelation extends, which must be religiously guarded and faithfully expounded (*LG* 25).

In this passage, "deposit of Revelation" seems to be referring to divinely revealed teaching of faith and morals. The section ends with the following statement:

> The Roman Pontiff and the bishops, in view of their office and the importance of the matter, by fitting means diligently strive to inquire properly into that revelation and to give apt expression to its contents; but a new public revelation they do not accept as pertaining to the divine deposit of faith (*LG* 25).

The phrase "deposit of faith" is used to describe judgments made by the Pope and/or bishops in union with him that are in accord with Revelation itself (Jesus). *Lumen Gentium* actually cross-references Vatican I, "Dogmatic Constitution I on the Church of Christ," for this sentence that uses "deposit of faith." Supernatural truths that are protected and passed down by the Magisterium are invoked by using the phrase "deposit of faith."

Gaudium et Spes, "The Pastoral Constitution on the Church in the Modern World," uses "deposit of faith" in a very similar manner. It states:

> Furthermore, theologians, within the requirements and methods proper to theology, are invited to seek continually for more suitable ways of communicating doctrine to the men of their times; for the deposit of Faith or the truths are one thing and the manner in which they are enunciated, in the same meaning and understanding, is another.[14] (*GS* 62)

The deposit is identified with "truths" or doctrinal teaching, which are permanent and unchanging. The way these supernatural truths are expressed can be improved upon, but the actual divine teachings do not change.

The last Vatican II document that uses the phrase "deposit of faith" is the "Decree on Ecumenism," *Unitatis Redintegratio*. The occurrence is in chapter 2, "The Practice of Ecumenism":

---

14   Cf. John XXIII, prayer delivered on Oct. 11, 1962, at the beginning of the council: AAS 54 (1962), 792.

Thus if, in various times and circumstances, there have been deficiencies in moral conduct or in church discipline, or even in the way that church teaching has been formulated—to be carefully distinguished from the deposit of faith itself—these can and should be set right at the opportune moment (*UR* 6).

Again the immutable nature of the deposit of faith is brought forth. The deposit is a reference to the contents of Church teaching. There is a distinction made between the formulation of Church teaching, which can be improved and therefore changed, and the actual teaching itself, which is constant.

Outside of *Dei Verbum*, the deposit of faith is unfailingly seen as divine teaching or supernatural truths that have been handed down in the life of the Church. This teaching is preserved against all error due to the promises given by Christ to the Church (cf. John 16:13; Matt. 16:18). If one only considered the uses of "deposit" in *Lumen Gentium, Unitatis Redintegratio,* and *Gaudium et Spes*, an identification of the deposit of faith with merely dogmatic formulations would be understandable. Given the nature and content of *Dei Verbum*, whenever the deposit of faith is discussed, it must be seen and understood through the lens of *Dei Verbum*. The divine teaching of the deposit of faith has to be seen as going beyond mere intellectual formulas and inclusive of all deeds and words of Christ and the inspiration of the Holy Spirit. The deposit of faith has to be viewed as going beyond mere words, given that its purpose is to embody and pass on Christ Himself. Sacred Scripture and Sacred Tradition are witnesses to the definitive Word!

CHAPTER 4

Post–Vatican II's Expression (John Paul II, *Catechism of the Catholic Church*)

—ᶬᶬ—

THIS CHAPTER WILL EXPLORE THE use of the phrase "deposit of faith" in postconciliar documents. The *Catechism of the Catholic Church*, documents from the pontificate of Pope John Paul II, and documents from various congregations will be examined in an effort to dig deeper into what the Church means when she uses the term "deposit" or "deposit of faith."

At the release of the first edition of the *Catechism of the Catholic Church* in 1992, an apostolic constitution was released with it. The title of this constitution was *Fidei Depositum*,[1] which is Latin for "deposit of faith." This was the first universal catechism in the Church's life since the Council of Trent in the sixteenth century. The *Catechism* was called for by a

---

1 Henceforth, this term will be referred to as simply *Depositum*.

synod of bishops that met in 1985 to celebrate the twentieth anniversary of Vatican II. *Fidei Depositum* acts as a kind of preface to the *Catechism*, which implicitly reveals what is meant by the phrase "deposit of faith." The *Catechism* is a sure reference point[2] for the teachings of the Catholic Church, and the *Catechism*'s preface, *Depositum*, seems to indicate that the phrase "deposit of faith" will more than likely be referencing sacred doctrine. The actual text of *Depositum* will now be explored.

Depositum begins with a discussion of the purpose of Vatican II. The document states the following:

> The principal task entrusted to the Council by Pope John XXIII was to guard and present better the precious *deposit* of Christian doctrine in order to make it more accessible to the Christian faithful and to all people of good will. For this reason the Council was not first of all to condemn the errors of the time, but above all to strive calmly to show the strength and beauty of the *doctrine of the faith*.[3]

There is an explicit and direct use of "deposit" in reference to Christian doctrine or teaching. The *Catechism* is a fulfillment of the Second Vatican

---

2 cf. Pope John Paull II, "Fidei Depositum," *Welcome to the Catholic Church*, CD-ROM (Harmony Media, 2007)(emphasis added).

3 Ibid.(emphasis added).

Council's desire to make the deposit more accessible to the faithful. In fact, the *Catechism* is described as a compendium of all Catholic doctrine regarding faith and morals.[4] One of the purposes of the *Catechism* is "for a catechesis renewed at the living sources of the faith"[5] The *Depositum* presents how doctrine should be presented, and this implicitly reveals the "living sources" of the faith that comprise and preserve the deposit:

> The presentation of doctrine must be biblical and liturgical...A catechism should faithfully and systematically present the teaching of Sacred Scripture, the living Tradition in the Church and the authentic Magisterium, as well as the spiritual heritage of the Fathers, Doctors, and saints of the Church, to allow for a better knowledge of the Christian mystery and for enlivening the faith of the People of God.[6]

The "living sources" of the faith are Sacred Scripture; the liturgy; the living Tradition in the Church; the authentic Magisterium; and the spiritual heritage of the fathers, doctors, and saints of the Church.

---

4   cf. Ibid.

5   Ibid.

6   Ibid.

At the release of the definitive edition of the *Catechism of the Catholic Church*, an apostolic letter, *Laetamur Magnopere*,[7] was also promulgated as a kind of preface. The letter states:

These conclusions, insofar as they allow for a better expression of the *Catechism*'s contents regarding the *deposit* of the Catholic faith, or enable certain *truths of this faith* to be formulated in a way more suited to the requirements of contemporary catechetical instruction, have been approved by me [Pope John Paul II] and thus have been incorporated into this Latin typical edition.[8]

The deposit of the Catholic faith is unambiguously referred to as "certain truths of this faith." Again, the focus is on doctrine. The letter adds another element to the deposit:

This text will provide every catechist with sound help for communicating the one, perennial *deposit of faith* within the local Church, while seeking, with the help of the Holy Spirit, to link the wondrous *unity of the*

---

7 Henceforth this term will be referred to as *Laetamur.*

8 Pope John Paull II, "Apostolic Letter Laetamur Magnopere," *Welcome to the Catholic Church*, CD-ROM (Harmony Media, 2007) (emphasis added).

Christian mystery with the varied needs and conditions of those to whom this message is addressed.[9]

This quote seems to connect the deposit of faith to dogmatic truths as well as to the Christian mystery, which is never exhausted by words or human understanding. In fact, the Christian mystery is shown through "deeds wrought by God in the history of salvation," which comes to a culmination in Christ Jesus (cf. *DV* 2).

In the actual text of the *Catechism of the Catholic Church*, "deposit" is mentioned twelve times.[10] Nine of those occurrences take place in the first part of the *Catechism*, which is dedicated to the "Profession of Faith." There is definitely a doctrinal emphasis being placed on the meaning of the "deposit of faith."

The first mention of "deposit" arises in the section that deals with private revelations, which is located in a larger article entitled "The Revelation of God." The *Catechism* states:

Throughout the ages, there have been so-called "private" revelations, some of which have been recognized by the authority of the

---

9 Ibid. (emphasis added).
10 Not counting the glossary entries.

Church. They do not belong, however, to the *deposit of faith.* It is not their role to improve or complete *Christ's definitive Revelation,* but to help live more fully by it in a certain period of history...Christian faith cannot accept "revelations" that claim to surpass or correct the *Revelation of which Christ is the fulfillment...* (*CCC* 67, emphasis added)

Christ's definitive revelation is the essence of the deposit of faith. Private revelations can never modify "Revelation of which Christ is the fulfillment" (*CCC* 67). Again, the person of Christ is being seen as the summit of God revealing Himself.

The next few occurrences of "deposit of faith" surface in article 2, entitled "The Transmission of Divine Revelation." Everything mentioned in this article has to be viewed in the light of its instrumental value in passing on Revelation itself, which is Christ Jesus.

In the section "The Interpretation of the Heritage of Faith," the *Catechism* states the following:

The apostles entrusted the *"Sacred deposit"* of the faith (*the depositum fidei*), contained in Sacred Scripture and Tradition, to the whole of the Church. "By adhering to [*this heritage*] the entire holy people, united to its pastors, remains always faithful to the *teaching of the*

> *apostles, to the brotherhood, to the breaking of bread
> and the prayers*" (*CCC* 84, emphasis added).

This quote is mainly taken from *Dei Verbum* 10. The deposit of faith is contained in the Sacred Scripture and Sacred Tradition and has been given to the Church. This heritage is explicitly identified with the deposit of faith in the *Catechism*'s glossary. The contents of this "heritage" are apostolic doctrines, the sacraments, moral life (the brotherhood), and prayers, which correspond to the very structure of the *Catechism* and the Church itself. Doctrines are an important part of the deposit of faith, but they are not the only part. The entire life of the Church is mysteriously wrapped in this deposit.

The *Catechism* goes on to quote from *DV* 10:

> Yet this Magisterium is not superior to the Word of God, but is its servant. It teaches only what has been handed on to it. At the divine command and with the help of the Holy Spirit, it listens to this devotedly, guards it with dedication, and expounds it faithfully. All that it proposes for belief as being divinely revealed is drawn from this single deposit of faith (*CCC* 86, emphasis added).

The deposit of faith is equated with the Word of God. This Word is served by the Magisterium—the bishops in union with the pope. This Word is passed down in the Church in written and unwritten forms, which has the purpose of transmitting the Word made flesh (cf. John 1:14).

In the "In Brief" section, which summarizes a particular segment, the *Catechism* again quotes *Dei Verbum* 10: "Sacred Tradition and Sacred Scripture make up a *single sacred deposit* of the Word of God" (DV 10), in which, as in a mirror, the pilgrim Church contemplates God, the source of all her riches" (*CCC* 97, emphasis added).

The deposit is described as "single," showing the interdependence of Sacred Scripture and Sacred Tradition. The Church uses this unified source to contemplate God.

In the section dealing with man's response to God, particularly the language of faith, the *Catechism* states the following: "The Church, 'the pillar and bulwark of the truth,' faithfully guards 'the faith which was once for all delivered to the saints.' She guards the memory of Christ's words; it is she who from generation to generation hands on the apostles' confession of faith" (*CCC* 171, emphasis added).

The word "deposit" is not explicitly used in this reference, but the reference to Jude 3 has traditionally been looked at as a reference to the deposit (*paradidōmi*). The deposit of faith is made up of the memory of Christ's words and the apostles' confession of faith. The teaching element of the deposit is dominant with this reference. In the same section, the *Catechism* goes on to quote St. Irenaeus:

> We guard with care *the faith that we have received from the Church*, for without ceasing, under the action of God's Spirit, this *deposit of great price*, as if in an excellent vessel, is constantly being renewed and causes the very vessel that contains it to be renewed (*CCC* 175, emphasis added).

Once more, "the faith" is identified with the deposit.

St. Gregory of Nazianzen is quoted as he identifies the deposit of faith with the profession of faith in the Trinity, which can indirectly be seen as an affirmation of the ancient creeds as being essential to the deposit, seeing that they have a Trinitarian structure (cf. *CCC* 256). A doctrinal focus is discovered again.

As the *Catechism* discusses the four marks of the Church in the profession of faith, the following quote surfaces:

The Church is apostolic because she is founded on the apostles, in three ways:

> She was and remains built on "the foundation of the Apostles," the witnesses chosen and sent on mission by Christ himself. With the help of the Spirit dwelling in her, the Church keeps and hands *on the teaching, the "good deposit," the salutary words she has heard from the apostles.*
>
> She continues to be taught, sanctified, and guided by the apostles until Christ's return, through their successors in pastoral office: the college of bishops, "assisted by priests, in union with the successor of Peter, the Church's supreme pastor" (*CCC* 857, emphasis added).

The deposit of faith is explicitly defined as apostolic teaching preserved in the life of the Church by the power of the Holy Spirit.

As the hierarchical nature of the Church is discussed, the following quote arises, which cross-references *LG* 25:

> When the Church through its supreme Magisterium proposes a doctrine "for belief as being divinely revealed," and as the teaching of Christ, the definitions "must be adhered to

with the obedience of faith." This infallibility extends as far as the *deposit of divine Revelation itself* (*CCC* 891, emphasis added).

Supernatural, divinely revealed doctrines are identified as the deposit that is protected under the charism of infallibility.

There are two instances of the term "deposit" being used in the third part of the *Catechism*, which deals with morality and life in Christ. The text states:

The Magisterium of the Pastors of the Church in moral matters is ordinarily exercised in catechesis and preaching, with the help of the works of theologians and spiritual authors. Thus from generation to generation, under the aegis and vigilance of the pastors, the "*deposit*" of Christian moral teaching has been handed on, a *deposit* composed of a characteristic body of rules, commandments, and virtues proceeding from faith in Christ and animated by charity. Alongside the Creed and the Our Father, the basis for this catechesis has traditionally been the Decalogue which sets out the principles of moral life valid for all men (*CCC* 2033, emphasis added).

In this case, the deposit refers to Christian moral teaching, specifically an organic unit of rules, commandments, and virtues. This section of the *Catechism* goes on to say:

> The supreme degree of participation in the authority of Christ is ensured by the charism of infallibility. This infallibility extends as far as does the *deposit of divine Revelation*; it also extends to all those elements of doctrine, including morals, without which the *saving truths of the faith* cannot be preserved, explained, or observed (*CCC* 2035, emphasis added).

The deposit is addressed as divine revelation, explicitly salvific truths of the faith pertaining to doctrine or morals.

Pope John Paul II officially uses the phrase "deposit" or "deposit of faith" several times in his pontificate. Shortly after the release of the first edition of the *Catechism*, John Paul II gave thanks for it in one of his annual letters to the priests. He writes:

> It is fitting to include in our thanksgiving this year a particular element of gratitude for the gift of the *Catechism of the Catholic Church*. This

text is a response to the mission which the Lord has entrusted to his Church: to guard the *deposit of faith* and to hand it down intact, with authority and loving concern, to coming generations...Indeed, in this summary of the *deposit of faith*, we can find an authentic and sure norm for teaching Catholic doctrine, for catechetical activity among the Christian people, for that "new evangelization" of which today's world has such immense need.[11]

The text of the *Catechism* is characterized as an act of the Church that guards the deposit. The deposit is primarily addressed as a body of teachings that is handed down through the generations. The *Catechism* is explicitly referred to as a summary of the deposit of faith. This deposit is a treasure.

In John Paul II's *Catechesi Tradendae* (*Catechesis in Our Time*), the pope delivers a beautiful message about the source of catechesis:

Catechesis will always draw its content from the living source of the Word of God transmitted in Tradition and the Scriptures, for "sacred Tradition and Sacred Scripture make up a single sacred deposit of the Word of

---

11 Pope John Paull II, "Letter of John Paul II to Priests Holy Thursday 1993," *Welcome to the Catholic Church*, CD-ROM (Harmony Media, 2007), #2(emphasis added).

God, which is entrusted to the Church," as was recalled by the Second Vatican Council, which desired that "the ministry of the word-pastoral preaching, catechetics and all forms of Christian instruction...(should be) healthily nourished and (should) thrive in holiness through the word of Scripture."[12]

In the above quote, the distinction between Revelation and the way it is transmitted is elucidated once again. The label of "deposit" is given to the transmitters of this Revelation: Sacred Scripture and Sacred Tradition. John Paul II continues to make this distinction in *Mulieris Dignitatem*, his apostolic letter on the dignity of women. He states, "The comparison Eve-Mary constantly recurs in the course of reflection on the deposit of faith received from divine Revelation."[13]

In his apostolic letter *Ad Tuendam Fidem*, he clearly identifies the deposit of faith as divinely revealed doctrines:

Canon 750 § 1. Those things are to be believed by divine and catholic faith which are contained in the word of God as it has

---

12 Pope John Paull II, "Catechesi Tradendae," *Welcome to the Catholic Church*, CD-ROM (Harmony Media, 2007), #27.
13 Pope John Paull II, "Mulieris Dignitatem," *Welcome to the Catholic Church*, CD-ROM (Harmony Media, 2007), #11.

been written or handed down by tradition, that is, in the single deposit of faith entrusted to the Church, and which are at the same time proposed as divinely revealed either by the solemn Magisterium of the Church, or by its ordinary and universal Magisterium, which in fact is manifested by the common adherence of Christ's faithful under the guidance of the sacred Magisterium. All are therefore bound to avoid any contrary doctrines.[14]

Things that are to be believed by divine and catholic faith make up the deposit of faith.

John Paul II perseveres in using deposit of faith to refer to divinely revealed teachings. Truth, dogma, truths of faith, truths contained in our venerable doctrine, and unity of faith briefly summarize the ways in which John Paul II uses deposit of faith.[15]

---

14 Pope John Paull II, "Apostolic Letter of Pope John Paul II Ad Tuendam Fidem By which Certain Norms are Inserted into the Code of Canon Law and into the Code of Canons of the Eastern Churches ISSUED 'MOTU PROPRIO,'" *Welcome to the Catholic Church*, CD-ROM (Harmony Media, 2007), #4.

15 Pope John Paull II, "Ut Unum Sint," *Welcome to the Catholic Church*, CD-ROM (Harmony Media, 2007), #18; Pope John Paull II, "Veritatis Splendor," *Welcome to the Catholic Church*, CD-ROM (Harmony Media, 2007); Pope John Paull II, "Sapientia Christiana Apostolic Constitution," *Welcome to the Catholic Church*, CD-ROM (Harmony Media, 2007); Pope John Paull II, "Pastor Bonus Apostolic Constitution of Pope John Paul II," *Welcome to the Catholic Church*, CD-ROM (Harmony Media, 2007).

Congregation documents will now be explored for usages of deposit of faith. Congregation for the Clergy's "General Directory for Catechesis" employs the phrase several times. The directory states:

> The Second Vatican Council set as one of its principal tasks the "better conservation and presentation of the precious deposit of Christian doctrine so as to render it more accessible to Christ's faithful and to all men of good will." The content of that deposit is the word of God which is safeguarded in the Church… The whole Tradition of the Church together with Scripture is contained in the "deposit of faith." "The sayings of the holy Fathers are a witness to the life-giving presence of this Tradition, showing how its riches are poured out in the practice and life of the Church, in her belief and in her prayer."[16]

Christian doctrine is recognized as being a main part of the deposit, but there is also an indication that the deposit of faith encompasses more than just "truths." "The whole Tradition of the Church with Scripture" expands the scope of the deposit of faith. The whole tradition of the Church includes not just

---

16 Congregation for the Clergy, "General Directory for Catechesis," *Welcome to the Catholic Church*, CD-ROM (Harmony Media, 2007), #125, #129.

doctrines but all sacraments, the moral life, and the covenant relationship of prayer as well. The directory also says:

> This "deposit of faith" is like the treasure of a householder; it is entrusted to the Church, the family of God, and she continuously draws from it things new and old. All God's children, animated by his Spirit, are nourished by this treasure of the Word. They know that the Word is Jesus Christ, the Word made man and that his voice continues to resound in the Church and in the world through the Holy Spirit. The Word of God, by wondrous divine "condescension" is directed toward us and reaches us by means of human "deeds and words," "just as the Word of the eternal Father, when he took on himself the flesh of human weakness, became like men." And so without ceasing to be the word of God, it is expressed in human words. Although close to us, it still remains veiled, in a "kenotic" state.[17]

This quote seems to be saying that the deposit of faith is ultimately Jesus or at least that the whole purpose behind the deposit is to communicate Jesus, the fullness of God's revelation. Jesus, the Word, is

---

17 Ibid.

transmitted to us through human deeds and words, which is definitely a reference to the Incarnation but extends to Sacred Scripture and Sacred Tradition, the very life of the Church.

The Sacred Congregation for the Doctrine of the Faith issued a document dedicated to theologians entitled "Instruction on the Ecclesial Vocation of the Theologian." This puts forth the duty and responsibility of theologians to serve the authentic teachers of the faith, the Magisterium. The document states:

> By its nature, the task of religiously guarding and loyally expounding the deposit of divine Revelation (in all its integrity and purity), implies that the Magisterium can make a pronouncement "in a definitive way" on propositions which, even if not contained among the truths of faith, are nonetheless intimately connected with them, in such a way, that the definitive character of such affirmations derives in the final analysis from revelation itself.[18]

The above quote definitely gives a doctrinally dominant tone to the deposit of faith. The congregation, in its "Instruction on Some Aspects of the Use of the Instruments of Social Communication in Promoting

---

18 Sacred Congregation for the Doctrine of Faith, "Instruction on the Ecclesial Vocation of the Theologian," *Welcome to the Catholic Church*, CD-ROM (Harmony Media, 2007), #16.

the Doctrine of Faith," applies the same tenor with its use of "sound doctrine."[19]

The Congregation of the Clergy implies a larger scope of content for the deposit of faith in their document "Priests in the New Testament." The document states:

> The Apostles handed on in their writings and by their spoken word (cf. 2 Thess. 2:15) everything that they had received from the Word of God made flesh.
>
> "Give the things you have heard from me in the presence of many witnesses to trustworthy persons who are capable of teaching also others" (2 Tim. 2:2).
>
> Such mission of "maintaining the deposit" (1 Tim. 6:20; 2 Tim. 1:14) must be exercised by the successors of the Apostles who have been charged through the imposition of hands (1 Tim. 4:14; 2 Tim 1:6; 1 Tim. 5:22).[20]

The apostles are handing on *everything* that they received from the Lord, Christ Jesus. Does this mean

19 cf. Sacred Congregation for the Doctrine of Faith, "Instruction on Some Aspects of the Use of the Instruments of Social Communication in Promoting the Doctrine of Faith," *Welcome to the Catholic Church*, CD-ROM (Harmony Media, 2007), #2.

20 Congregation for the Clergy, "Priests in the New Testament," *Welcome to the Catholic Church*, CD-ROM (Harmony Media, 2007).

that they are simply handing on the doctrinal truths of the faith? They have handed on much more. They received His very life.

The postconciliar documents examined show a doctrinally focused meaning by the usage of the phrase "deposit of faith" or simply "deposit." Permanent and universal teachings of faith and morals are stressed. Given the relativistic atmosphere the world is in, this focus is understandable and critical. Sacred Scripture and Sacred Tradition are the single sources from which these eternal truths are drawn. To limit the deposit of faith to simply a group of dogmatic definitions would undercut the true value of Christ's treasure that he gave to the world. While the dominant tone of these documents stresses supernatural truths, these faith and moral truths serve a greater purpose of bringing the world into contact with Revelation itself, Christ Jesus. Not only does the profession of faith compose the deposit of faith, but the sacraments, the moral life, and prayer are included as well. The living Tradition (including the Sacred Scriptures) of the Church is really the heart of the deposit that connects believers to Christ Jesus. This living Tradition is everything the apostles received from the Lord and His Spirit, and they received no less than the Master's life mediated to them through His mystical body, the Church.

CHAPTER 5

Importance for Modern
Catholic Life and Doctrine

—⟋⟍—

THIS CHAPTER WILL EXPLORE THE importance of the
deposit of faith for modern Catholic theology and
life. The deposit of faith plays a critical role in both.
Catholic theology will be addressed first.

Catholic theology can be described as "faith seeking understanding."[1] St. Augustine writes, "Faith
seeks, understanding finds; whence the prophet says,
'Unless ye believe, ye shall not understand'" (Isa.
7:9).[2] In these statements, faith is mentioned first
for a very important reason. Faith, a gift from God,
must precede every endeavor of human understanding that is described as theology. This precedence ap-

---

1 Sidney Norton Anselm, Saint, Archbishop of Canterbury; Deane,
*Proslogium; Monologium; an Appendix, in Behalf of the Fool, by Gaunilon;
and Cur Deus Homo* (Bellingham, WA: Logos Bible Software, 2009),
#2.

2 Philip Schaff, *The Nicene and Post-Nicene Fathers, Vol. III* (Oak
Harbor: Logos Research Systems, 1997), 200.

plies to faith in its subjective and objective senses. A Catholic theologian must first of all be a believer! The subjective sense of faith is found in the interior life of a person: "The commitment to theology requires a spiritual effort to grow in virtue and holiness."[3] Faith as an object must also precede any theology. The deposit of faith has an objective dimension to it: the body of divinely revealed doctrines. These doctrines act as first principles in the science of theology. "The Instruction for Theologians" states:

> In theology this freedom of inquiry is the hallmark of a rational discipline whose object is given by Revelation, handed on and interpreted in the Church under the authority of the Magisterium, and received by faith. These givens have the force of principles. To eliminate them would mean to cease doing theology.[4]

The deposit of faith plays such an essential role in theology that without it the activity of seeking understanding cannot even be described as theology.

The theologian seeks to fulfill the command from Sacred Scripture: "But in your hearts reverence

---

3   Sacred Congregation for the Doctrine of Faith, "Instruction on the Ecclesial Vocation of the Theologian," #9.

4   Ibid., Synthesis of document.

Christ as Lord. Always be prepared to make a defense to anyone who calls you to account for the hope that is in you, yet do it with gentleness and reverence" (1 Pet. 3:15). Deepening the understanding of the Word of God passed down in the Church through Sacred Scripture and Sacred Tradition is the vocation of the theologian. The "Instruction for Theologians" states:

> His role is to pursue in a particular way an ever deeper understanding of the Word of God found in the inspired Scriptures and handed on by the living Tradition of the Church. He does this in communion with the Magisterium which has been charged with the responsibility of preserving the deposit of faith...
> Theology, for its part, gains, by way of reflection, an ever deeper understanding of the Word of God found in the Scripture and handed on faithfully by the Church's living Tradition under the guidance of the Magisterium. Theology strives to clarify the teaching of Revelation with regard to reason and gives it finally an organic and systematic form.[5]

Theologians must see their roles as a service to the Magisterium, the authentic teachers and preservers

---

5   Ibid., #6, #21.

of the faith. No theologian ever "graduates" from the material in the *Catechism of the Catholic Church*: "The magisterium is an indispensable help to theology by its authentic transmission of the deposit of faith..."[6]

The deposit of faith plays an essential role in a healthy and fruitful Catholic life. Human beings are made by God and for Him who is truth (cf. John 14:6). This is why every human being seeks the truth about him- or herself and his or her purpose. Unfortunately, this search is often slowed and derailed due to the spiritually toxic atmosphere of the world. According to Cardinal Ratzinger, human beings are living in a dictatorship of relativism.[7] Nothing can be known with any definitiveness. Absolute truth is seen as obsolete and outdated. In order to be accepted according to modernity, one must drown in the sea of opinions. The deposit of faith is the life raft for every Catholic and, in fact, every human being who seeks truth and meaning in life: "Truth, by its nature, seeks to be communicated since man was created for the perception of truth and from the depths of his being desires

---

6   International Theological Commission, ed., "Theology Today: Perspectives, Principles and Criteria" (International Theological Commission's page on the Vatican website, March 8, 2012), http://www.vatican.va/roman_curia/congregations/cfaith/cti_documents/rc_cti_doc_20111129_teologia-oggi_en.html.

7   cf. "Pope Benedict XVI," n.d., http://www.ewtn.com/pope/words/conclave_homily.asp, (accessed November 15, 2011).

knowledge of it so that he can discover himself in the truth and find there his salvation" (cf. 1 Tim. 2:4).[8]

The deposit of faith is the teaching of Jesus, and the Holy Spirit preserves it in the life of the Church. A Catholic dictionary states that the deposit of faith is the "body of revelation, containing truths to be believed and principles of conduct, which was given by Christ to the Apostles, to be preserved by them and their successors, with the guarantee of infallibility, for the guidance of the Church."[9] This body of revelation is absolute and unchanging. This Divine truth has been often referred to as the rule of faith.[10] The Pontifical Council for Promoting Christian Unity states that the deposit of faith itself is equivalent to the truths that are contained in the venerable doctrine.[11] This truth is what marks and sets apart Catholic Christianity: "following the fundamental significance which the Church always attached to

---

8   Sacred Congregation for the Doctrine of Faith, "Instruction on the Ecclesial Vocation of the Theologian," #7.

9   Donald Attwater, *A Catholic Dictionary (The Catholic Encyclopedic Dictionary)*, 2nd ed. (New York: Macmillan Co., 1949), 143.

10   cf. Saint; Fathers of the English Dominican Province Thomas Aquinas, *Summa Theologica*, Complete English ed. (Bellingham, WA: Logos Bible Software, 2009), STh., II–II q.2 a.6 ad.3.

11   cf. Pontifical Council for Promoting Christian Unity, "Directory for the Application of Ecumenism," *Welcome to the Catholic Church*, CD-ROM (Harmony Media, 2007), #74.

this deposit of faith as the very basis and the characterizing feature of the true religion of Christ."[12]

Infallible truth is given in the deposit of faith and also in the historical or logical truths intimately connected to the deposit. The Congregation for the Doctrine of the Faith issued a commentary on the concluding formula of the Profession of Faith in 1998, which makes this clear. The Profession of Faith ends with three propositions. The first proposition deals with believing "everything contained in the Word of God, whether written or handed down in Tradition, which the Church, either by a solemn judgment or by the ordinary and universal Magisterium, sets forth to be believed as divinely revealed."[13] The second proposition deals with definitive teachings, and the third references nondefinitive, yet still magisterial, teachings. The CDF's commentary on the second proposition is extremely helpful in seeing how infallible truth cannot be confined to the deposit of faith:

The second proposition of the *Professio fidei* states: "I also firmly accept and hold each and everything definitively proposed by the

---

12 Manlio Simonetti, *Biblical Interpretation in the Early Church : An Historical Introduction to Patristic Exegesis* (Edinburgh: T&T Clark, 1994), 120–21.

13 Congregation for the Doctrine of the Faith, "Profession of Faith and the Oath of Fidelity on Assuming an Office to Be Exercised in the Name of the Church," *L'Osservatore Romano,* July 15, 1998.

Church regarding teaching on faith and morals." The object taught by this formula includes *all those teachings belonging to the dogmatic or moral area, which are necessary for faithfully keeping and expounding the deposit of faith, even if they have not been proposed by the Magisterium of the Church as formally revealed...* Every believer, therefore, is required to give *firm and definitive assent* to these truths, based on faith in the Holy Spirit's assistance to the Church's Magisterium, and on the Catholic doctrine of the infallibility of the Magisterium in these matters.[14]

From this commentary, the reader is informed that the first proposition deals with the deposit of faith. The second proposition is not dealing with the deposit or divine revelation but with definitive faith or moral teaching that must be assented to based on the Holy Spirit's assistance and the infallibility of the Magisterium.

The deposit of faith preserves the prophetic voice of Jesus, who is the Truth (cf. John 14:6) for the faithful today. Joseph Pohle, in his treatise on Redemption, comments:

---

14 Congregation for the Doctrine of the Faith, "Doctrinal Commentary on the Concluding Formula of the Professio Fidei," *L'Osservatore Romano,* July 15, 1998.

The very fact that Christ established a Church to teach "all nations" shows that He wished her to continue His prophetical office. He guaranteed her His special assistance and promised to be with her "all days, even to the consummation of the world." Having established her as a teacher, He sent her the Spirit of Truth, who informs and vivifies her as the soul informs and actuates the body, and enables her to keep the *deposit of faith* intact against all attempts at diminution or distortion. Thus the infallibility of the Church and of her Supreme Pontiff ultimately rests upon the prophetic office of Christ Himself, who is the infallible source and teacher of all truth.[15]

This preserved truth, which rests on Christ as prophet, is not merely logical but salvific truth. Jesus says, "And you will know the truth, and the truth will make you free" (John 8:32). The Sacred Congregation for the Doctrine of the Faith states, "The truth which sets us free is a gift of Jesus Christ."[16] The Magisterium of the Church and theology have the common goal of

---

15   Arthur Pohle, Joseph; Preuss, *Soteriology: A Dogmatic Treatise on the Redemption* (St. Louis, MO: B. Herder, 1919), 146–47 (emphasis added).

16   Sacred Congregation for the Doctrine of Faith, "Instruction on the Ecclesial Vocation of the Theologian," #1.

enabling the people of God to experience this free-dom: "The living Magisterium of the Church and theology, while having different gifts and functions, ultimately have the same goal: preserving the People of God in the truth which sets free and thereby mak-ing them 'a light to the nations.'"[17] *The New Dictionary of Theology* addresses the deposit of faith as "salvif-ic knowledge which God communicated through Jesus."[18]

The people of God abide in freedom by being rooted in the truth. This truth is ultimately the Second Person of the Trinity. Freedom is not derived from doing whatever one decides to do but by being in communion with the Lord. This is the practical purpose of the deposit of faith. The deposit of faith is a means through which the faithful are brought into the presence and life of the Trinity. The Apostle John's first letter is very telling: "Let what you heard from the beginning abide in you. If what you heard from the beginning abides in you, then you will abide in the Son and in the Father. And this is what he has promised us, eternal life" (1 John 2:24–25). There is an intimate connection between what the disciple hears (the truth) and his or her abiding in God Himself. The Sacred Congregation for the

---

17 Ibid., #21.

18 Joseph A Komonchak, "Deposit of Faith," *The New Dictionary of Theology* (Collegeville, Minn: Michael Glazier, The Liturgical Press, 1987), 1,112.

Doctrine of Faith states, "In the Christian faith, knowledge and life, truth and existence are intrinsically connected."[19]

Christ Jesus intends for the faithful to live in Him through the heritage of faith He has deposited in His mystical body, which is the Church. When one considers the entire history of how the term "deposit of faith" has been used, dogma is at the forefront, but a more accurate description would be the heritage of faith, which has, at its center, the Paschal Mystery and everything Jesus did and said. It is this inclusive definition of the deposit of faith—which includes not only salvific doctrinal statements but the entire experience of Jesus as well, which contains elements that cannot be reduced to writing or doctrinal statements—that has to be understood as connecting the faithful to the life of God. *The New Catholic Encyclopedia* states:

> The deposit of faith includes *all that God has entrusted to the Church* in their enduring salvific efficacy and in their divinely revealed meaning, and the prolongation of that reality and meaning in the Church by means of the divinely given Sacraments, Scriptures, hierarchical institution, and the continuous

---

19 Sacred Congregation for the Doctrine of Faith, "Instruction on the Ecclesial Vocation of the Theologian," #1.

> interpretative assistance of the Holy Spirit in
> the whole body of the faithful.[20]

The deposit of faith is nothing less than the life of Christ passed down to us through the life of the Church and through the means of the body of truths preserved in the Scripture and Tradition. It is authoritatively interpreted and thus preserved by the Holy Spirit-led Magisterium. *The Modern Catholic Encyclopedia* states, "The deposit is first and foremost God's saving presence in history. Every expression of this foundational mystery, where in Scripture or tradition, is a more or less successful attempt to give verbal expression to this ultimate reality."[21] God's saving presence in history culminates in Christ Jesus. *Our Sunday Visitor's Catholic Encyclopedia* states that the deposit of faith is of great value: "The treasure of saving truth, in itself nothing other than Christ Himself, contains the definitive revelation of God's inner life and of his intentions in our regard."[22] Nunier and Dupius reveal this same insight: the deposit of faith being God's own life.[23]

---

20   Chirico, "New Catholic Encyclopedia," 675 (emphasis added).

21   William McFadden, "Deposit of Faith," ed. Glazier and Hellwig, *The Modern Catholic Encyclopedia* (Collegeville, Minn: Liturgical Press, 1994), 238.

22   Peter M. J Stravinskas, *Our Sunday Visitor's Catholic Encyclopedia* (Our Sunday Visitor Pub., c1991), 300.

23   cf. Dupuis, *The Christian Faith*, 35.

More support is given for this connection between the deposit of faith and the presence of God in the following quote from John Henry Cardinal Newman:

> But a great *Pontiff must be detached from every-thing save the deposit of faith*, the tradition of the Apostles, and the vital principles of the divine polity. He may use, he may uphold, he may and will be very slow to part with, a hundred things which have grown up, or taken shelter, or are stored, under the shadow of the Church; but, at bottom, and after all, he will be simply detached from pomp and etiquette, secular rank, secular learning, schools and libraries, Basilicas and Gothic cathedrals, old ways, old alliances, and old friends. He will be rightly jealous of their loss, but still *he will "know nothing but" Him whose Vicar he is*; he will not stake his fortunes, he will not rest his cause, upon any one else—this is what he will do, and what he will not do, as in fact the great Popes of history have shown, in their own particular instances, on so many and various occasions.[24]

Cardinal Newman, in his description of characteristics of the Pope, draws a kind of parallel between

---

24 John Henry Newman, *Historical sketches, Volume 3* (London: Basil Montagu Pickering, 1872), 133 (emphasis added).

the deposit of faith, which the Pope must always be attached to, and "Him" who is the Lord. There is an implicit connection between the deposit of faith and the presence of Christ. The New Testament Scripture scholar Peter Williamson gives a very telling commentary on the use of the adjective "living" in reference to Tradition, which is an essential element of the deposit of faith. He writes:

> The word "Tradition" is often modified in the *IB*[C] by the adjectives "living" (8x) and "great" (5x). When the *IB*[C] describes Tradition as "living," it emphasizes its contemporary and vital presence in the Church, and that it consists of more than "a mere communication of individual truths but as the life-bestowing presence of God's word."[25]

The Tradition cannot be reduced to a mere communication of truths but is the mechanism through which the presence of God is delivered.

In the "Instruction on the Ecclesial Vocation of the Theologian," this connection between the deposit of faith and the presence of God is also made. The text states:

---

25 Peter Williamson, *Catholic Principles for Interpreting Scripture: A Study of the Pontifical Biblical Commission's the Interpretation of the Bible in the Church*, vol. 22 (Roma: Pontificio Istituto biblico, 2001), 139.

> When God gives Himself to man as a friend, man becomes free, in accordance with the Lord's word: "No longer do I call you servants, for the servant does not know what his master is doing; but I have called you friends, for all that I have heard from my Father I have made known to you" (John 15:15).[26]

There is an implicit connection between God giving Himself to man and His revealing "all that I heard from the Father." The Lord calls the faithful "friends" (i.e., sharing His personal presence) because of His revelation to them from the Father. This revelation—or, in other words, the deposit of faith—brings about the presence of God as a friend. "The Instruction" also states the following: "The acts of assent and submission to the Word entrusted to the Church under the guidance of the Magisterium are directed ultimately to Him and lead us into the realm of true freedom."[27] An intimate connection is implied between the Word entrusted to the Church (the deposit) and Him (Christ). The deposit of faith is meant to stir one's faith that God's presence may be more realized in the life of the faithful:

---

26 Sacred Congregation for the Doctrine of Faith, "Instruction on the Ecclesial Vocation of the Theologian," #1.

27 Ibid., #41.

In order to exercise the prophetic function in the world, the People of God must continually reawaken or "rekindle" its own life of faith (cf. 2 Tim. 1:6). It does this particularly by contemplating ever more deeply, under the guidance of the Holy Spirit, the contents of the faith itself and by dutifully presenting the reasonableness of the faith to those who ask for an account of it (cf. 1 Pet. 3:15).[28]

Historically speaking, "the rule of faith" was often the phrase used to describe the reality that is now spoken of as the deposit of faith. Two terms that described the rule of faith were "ultimate or remote" and "proximate." The ultimate rule of faith refers to the truthfulness of God in revealing Himself, while the proximate rule of faith references the Bible, Tradition, and the serving Magisterium.[29] The proximate rule of faith is the means through which the faithful encounter the truthfulness of God, which is inseparable from His presence given His simplicity. The phrase "deposit of faith" is now being used, especially since Vatican II, to include both the proximate and remote aspects of the rule of faith.

---

28   Ibid., #5.

29   cf. Hugh Pope, "The Rule of Faith," *Catholic Encyclopedia*, n.d., http://www.newadvent.org/cathen/05766b.htm, (accessed June 15, 2011).

The deposit of faith is an essential part of fruitful Catholic theology and life. Theology cannot even be considered authentic theology if the endeavor does not use the deposit of faith as its first principle. Theology has the primary goal of deepening the faithful's understanding of the deposit of faith given by God. A theologian's academic freedom is not hampered by the deposit of faith; rather, it is grounded and enabled to reach new heights. Catholic life is preserved from the toxic atmosphere of relativism through the preservation of the deposit of faith. The prophetic voice of Jesus is preserved and passed down in the life of the Church so that the world would receive the truth and, as a result, be set free. This truth is not merely intellectual but salvific, given that the truth is ultimately a Divine Person. Abiding in God's presence is achieved through the means of the deposit of faith. The deposit of faith is exceedingly important in Catholic theology and life.

Conclusion

—⁓⁓—

THE MEANING OF THE PHRASE "deposit of faith" or "deposit" has been examined throughout its understanding in the life of the Church. In the term's infancy stage in the Sacred Scripture and with the early Church writers, the deposit was a reference to written or oral divinely revealed doctrines and morals, often referred to as the "rule of faith." The Church's creeds were often identified with this deposit, which was not merely words or ordinances, but one that had a salvific and nourishing instrumentality.

In papal encyclicals and ecumenical councils prior to the Second Vatican Council, the meaning of "deposit of faith" was the Word of God or divine teaching from Jesus and the Holy Spirit, transmitted to the apostles and passed down in the life of the Church. The deposit continues to include faith and morals as well as the two forms of written and oral teaching. The doctrine is not merely "head knowledge" but must be seen as a means through which the faithful can experience the living Lord.

The Second Vatican Council's Dogmatic Constitution on Divine Revelation (*Dei Verbum*) sets the tone for every other reference to the "deposit" in the council's documents. *Dei Verbum* gives the nature of divine revelation itself, which is a Divine Person! It proceeds from this starting point to teaching how this Revelation is transmitted in the life of the Church. This transmission comes though the deposit of faith, which comes to the faithful from one divine wellspring. The heart of the deposit is not just dogmatic formulas but the deeds and words of Christ as well. The oral and written forms are shown as interpenetrating one another, which renders questions about "two sources" less important. The purpose of the deposit is to embody and pass on Christ Himself. Other references to the "deposit" in the Vatican II documents portray the meaning of divine teaching or supernatural truths. These other references must be seen through the lens of *Dei Verbum*.

The *Catechism of the Catholic Church*, documents from the pontificate of St. Pope John Paul the Great, and congregation documents show a doctrinal focus with respect to the "deposit of faith." But what is at the heart of the deposit of faith is the living Tradition, which includes not only the profession of faith but also the sacraments, the moral life, and prayer. The deposit of faith serves a greater purpose of bringing the world into contact with the Lord of Lords.

Catholic theology and life are preserved through the great gift of the deposit of faith. Jesus, who is the truth, sets the world free through His deposit. From the theologian to the infant, meaning of life and purpose can be achieved and passed down despite the culture, which attempts to pull humans away from God.

The usage of the phrase "deposit of faith" has grown in the life of the Church. The meanings behind the phrase have been varied yet ultimately consistent with one another. Divine revelation is definitely the dominant meaning, but this revelation can never be approached as mere dogmatic formulations. The Church has consistently reminded the faithful that it is not a religion of the book but of the Person of Christ (cf. *CCC* 108). The faithful can never be satisfied with head knowledge of the doctrine and morals. Unfortunately, this has happened, given the testimony of people who have left the Church because they "found Jesus." God's teachings have always had the purpose of bringing the world into communion with Him.

BIBLIOGRAPHY

Addis, W. E. and Arnold, T. "Deposit of Faith." in *Catholic Dictionary: Containing Some Account of the Doctrine, Discipline, Rites, Ceremonies, Councils, and Religious Orders of the Catholic Church.* 9th ed. St. Louis, MO.: B. Herder, 1917.

Anselm, Saint, Archbishop of Canterbury, and Sidney Norton Deane. *Proslogium; Monologium; An Appendix, in Behalf of the Fool, by Gaunilon; and Cur Deus Homo.* Bellingham, WA: Logos Bible Software, 2009.

Attwater, Donald. *A Catholic Dictionary (The Catholic Encyclopedic Dictionary)* 2nd ed. New York, Macmillan Co., 1949.

Basil the Great, St. "Letter 105" in *The Faith Database.* CD-ROM. Third Millennium Media, 2008.

———. "Letter 242." *The Faith Database.* CD-ROM. Third Millennium Media, 2008.

Berardino, Angelo [ed.]; Quasten, Johannes [intro.] di. *Patrology. Volume IV. The Golden Age of Latin Patristic Literature from the Council of Nicea to the Council of Chalcedon.* Reprint. Allen, Texas, Christian Classic Inc., 1991.

Board, Confraternity of Christian Doctrine. Board of Trustees; Catholic Church. National Conference of Catholic Bishops; United States Catholic Conference. Administrative. *The New American Bible: Translated from the original languages with critical use of all the ancient sources and the revised New Testament.* Confraternity of Christian Doctrine, 1996.

Braman, Brian J. "Opinion polls and the deposit of faith." *Homiletic and Pastoral Review* 87 (November 1986): 65–69.

Brown, Raymond Edward, Fitzmyer, Joseph A., and Murphy, Roland Edmund. *The Jerome Biblical commentary.* Englewood Cliffs, NJ: Prentice-Hall, 1996.

Cassian, John. "Conference 14." *The Faith Database.* CD-ROM. Third Millennium Media, 2008.

Chirico, P. F. "Deposit of Faith." *New Catholic Encyclopedia.* Washington DC, Gale Group in association with the Catholic University of America, 2003.

Chrysostom, St. John. "Homily 11 on First Timothy." *The Faith Database.* CD-ROM. Third Millennium Media, 2008.

———. "Homily 11 on the Acts of the Apostles ACTS IV. 23." *The Faith Database*. CD-ROM. Third Millennium Media, 2008.

———. "Homily 12 on the Statues." *The Faith Database*. CD-ROM. Third Millennium Media, 2008.

———. "Homily 38 on First Corinthians." *The Faith Database*. CD-ROM. Third Millennium Media, 2008.

———. "Instructions to Catechumens." *The Faith Database*. CD-ROM. Third Millennium Media, 2008.

———. "Second Homily on Eutropius (After His Captivity)." *The Faith Database*. CD-ROM. Third Millennium Media, 2008.

Church, Catholic. *Vatican II Documents*. Vatican City: Libreria Editrice Vaticana, 2011.

Congar, Yves. *Tradition and Traditions: The Biblical, Historical, and Theological Evidence for Catholic Teaching on Tradition* 2nd ed. Ginn Pr, 1997.

Congregation for the Clergy. "General Directory for Catechesis." *Welcome to the Catholic Church*. CD-ROM. Harmony Media, 2007.

———. "Priests in the New Testament." *Welcome to the Catholic Church*. CD-ROM. Harmony Media, 2007.

Congregation for the Doctrine of the Faith. "Doctrinal Commentary on the Concluding Formula of the Professio Fidei." *L'Osservatore Romano*, July 15, 1998.

———. "Profession of Faith and the Oath of Fidelity on Assuming an Office to Be Exercised in the Name of the Church." *L'Osservatore Romano*, July 15, 1998.

Cyril of Jerusalem, St. "Catechetical Lecture 12." *The Faith Database*. CD-ROM. Third Millennium Media, 2008.

———. "Catechetical Lecture 5." *The Faith Database*. CD-ROM. Third Millennium Media, 2008.

Dupuis, Jacques. *The Christian Faith: In the Doctrinal Documents of the Catholic Church* 7th rev. Alba House, 2001.

Leo the Great, St. "Sermon 85." *The Faith Database*. CD-ROM. Third Millennium Media, 2008.

———. "Sermon 95." *The Faith Database*. CD-ROM. Third Millennium Media, 2008.

Gregory Nazianzen, St. "Oration 40." *The Faith Database.* CD-ROM. Third Millennium Media, 2008.

Gregory of Nyssa, St. "Answer to Eunomius' Second Book." *The Faith Database.* CD-ROM. Third Millennium Media, 2008.

Hahn, Scott W. *Kinship by Covenant: A Canonical Approach to the Fulfillment of God's Saving Promises.* New Haven; London: Yale University Press, 2009.

Hahnenberg. *Concise Guide to the Documents of Vatican II.* Cincinnati, Ohio: St. Anthony Messenger Press, 2007.

Hassett, Maurice. "John Cassian." *Catholic Encyclopedia.* The Faith Database CD-ROM. Third Millennium Media, 2008.

Hippolytus. "The AntiChrist." *The Faith Database.* CD-ROM. Third Millennium Media, 2008.

International Theological Commission, ed. "Theology Today: Perspectives, Principles and Criteria." International Theological Commission's page on the Vatican website, March 8, 2012. http://www.vatican.va/roman_curia/congregations/cfaith/cti_documents/rc_cti_doc_20111129_teologia-oggi_en.html.

Kirsch, J. P. "Hippolytus of Rome, Saint." *Catholic Encyclopedia.* The Faith Database CD-Rom. Third Millenium Media, 2008.

Kittel, Gerhard, Friedrich Gerhard, and Geoffrey William Bromiley. *Theological Dictionary of the New Testament.* Grand Rapids, MI: W. B. Eerdmans, 1985.

Komonchak, Joseph A. "Deposit of Faith." *The New Dictionary of Theology.* Collegeville, Minn: Michael Glazier, The Liturgial Press, 1987.

Latourelle. *Theology of Revelation: Including a Commentary on the Constitution "Dei Verbum" of Vatican II.* Staten Island, NY: Alba House, 1966.

McFadden, William, S. J. "Deposit of Faith." ed. Glazier and Hellwig. *The Modern Catholic Encyclopedia.* Collegeville, Minn: Liturgical Press, 1994.

de Moulins-Beaufort, E. "Henri de Lubac : Reader of Dei Verbum." *Communion/International Catholic Review* 28, no. 4 (2001): 669–694.

Newman, John Henry. *Historical Sketches, Volume 3.* London: Basil Montagu Pickering, 1872.

Nicholas Rademacher. "Deposit of Faith." ed. Glazier and Hellwig. *The Modern Catholic Encyclopedia*. Collegeville, Minn: Liturgical Press, c2004.

Norris, T. "On Revisiting Dei Verbum." *Irish Theological Quarterly* 66, no. 4 (2001): 315–337.

Orchard, Bernard. *A Catholic Commentary on Holy Scripture*. Toronto; New York; Edinburgh: Nelson, 1953.

Pius IX. "The False Freedom of Science (against James Frohschammer)." ed. Denzinger. *Welcome to the Catholic Church*. CD-ROM. Harmony Media, 2007.

Pohle, Joseph, and Arthur Preuss. *Soteriology: A Dogmatic Treatise on the Redemption*. St. Louis, MO: B. Herder, 1919.

Pontifical Council for Promoting Christian Unity. "Directory for the Application of Ecumenism." *Welcome to the Catholic Church*. CD-ROM. Harmony Media, 2007.

"Pope Benedict XVI," n.d. http://www.ewtn.com/pope/words/conclave_homily.asp. (accessed November 15, 2011).

Pope Clement XIII. "On the Dangers of Anti-Christian Writings." *The Faith Database.* CD-ROM. Third Millennium Media, 2008.

Pope Clement XIV. "Proclaiming a Universal Jubilee." *The Faith Database.* CD-ROM. Third Millennium Media, 2008.

Pope Gregory XVI. "Condemnation of the Works of George Hermes." ed. Denzinger. *Welcome to the Catholic Church.* CD-ROM. Harmony Media, 2007.

————. "On the 'Pragmatic Constitution." *The Faith Database.* CD-ROM. Third Millennium Media, 2008.

Pope, Hugh. "The Rule of Faith." *Catholic Encyclopedia,* n.d. http://www.newadvent.org/cathen/05766b. htm. (accessed June 15, 2011).

Pope John Paull II. "Apostolic Letter Laetamur Magnopere." *Welcome to the Catholic Church.* CD-ROM. Harmony Media, 2007.

————. "Apostolic Letter of Pope John Paul II Ad Tuendam Fidem By which Certain Norms are Inserted into the Code of Canon Law and into the Code of Canons of the Eastern Churches IS-SUED 'MOTU PROPRIO.'" *Welcome to the Catholic Church.* CD-ROM. Harmony Media, 2007.

————. "Catechesi Tradendae." *Welcome to the Catholic Church.* CD-ROM. Harmony Media, 2007.

————. "Fidei Depositum." *Welcome to the Catholic Church.* CD-ROM. Harmony Media, 2007.

————. "Letter of John Paul II to Priests Holy Thursday 1993." *Welcome to the Catholic Church.* CD-ROM. Harmony Media, 2007.

————. "Mulieris Dignitatem." *Welcome to the Catholic Church.* CD-ROM. Harmony Media, 2007.

————. "Pastor Bonus Apostolic Constitution of Pope John Paul II." *Welcome to the Catholic Church.* CD-ROM. Harmony Media, 2007.

————. "Sapientia Christiana Apostolic Constitution." *Welcome to the Catholic Church.* CD-ROM. Harmony Media, 2007.

————. "Ut Unum Sint." *Welcome to the Catholic Church.* CD-ROM. Harmony Media, 2007.

———. "Veritatis Splendor." *Welcome to the Catholic Church.* CD-ROM. Harmony Media, 2007.

Pope John XXIII. "Message of Peace." *Welcome to the Catholic Church.* CD-ROM. Harmony Media, 2007.

Pope Leo XIII. "Divinum Illud Munus." *Welcome to the Catholic Church.* CD-ROM. Harmony Media, 2007.

Pope Pius IX. "Ineffabilis Deus." *Welcome to the Catholic Church.* CD-ROM. Harmony Media, 2007.

Pope Pius VI. "Problems of the Pontificate." *The Faith Database.* CD-ROM. Third Millennium Media, 2008.

Pope Pius VII. "Return to Gospel Principles." *The Faith Database.* CD-ROM. Third Millennium Media, 2008.

Pope Pius X. "Editae Saepe." *Welcome to the Catholic Church.* CD-ROM. Harmony Media, 2007.

———. "Pascendi Dominici Gregis." *Welcome to the Catholic Church.* CD-ROM. Harmony Media, 2007.

Pope Pius XI. "Mortalium Animos." *Welcome to the Catholic Church.* CD-ROM. Harmony Media, 2007.

———. "Quadragesimo Anno." *Welcome to the Catholic Church.* CD-ROM. Harmony Media, 2007.

Pope Pius XII. "Humani Generis." *Welcome to the Catholic Church.* CD-ROM. Harmony Media, 2007.

———. "Mediator Dei (on the Sacred Liturgy)." *The Faith Database.* CD-ROM. Third Millennium Media, 2008.

———. "Munificentissimus Deus." *Welcome to the Catholic Church.* CD-ROM. Harmony Media, 2007.

Quasten, Johannes. *Patrology. Volume 2: The Ante-Nicene Literature After Irenaeus. Volume 2 Only.* Newman Press, 1953.

Ratzinger, Joseph. "Dogmatic Constitution on Divine Revelation." ed. Herbert Vorgrimler. *Commentary on the Documents of Vatican II.* New York, NY: Crossroad, 1989.

Sacred Congregation for the Doctrine of Faith. "Instruction on Some Aspects of the Use of the Instruments of Social Communication in Promoting the Doctrine of Faith." *Welcome to the Catholic Church.* CD-ROM. Harmony Media, 2007.

———. "Instruction on the Ecclesial Vocation of the Theologian." *Welcome to the Catholic Church.* CD-ROM. Harmony Media, 2007.

Schaff, Philip. *The Nicene and Post-Nicene Fathers, Vol. III.* Oak Harbor: Logos Research Systems, 1997.

Simonetti, Manlio. *Biblical Interpretation in the Early Church : An Historical Introduction to Patristic Exegesis.* Edinburgh: T&T Clark, 1994.

St. Irenaeus of Lyons. "Adversus Haereses (Book III, Chapter 24)." *The Faith Database.* CD-ROM. Third Millennium Media, 2008.

———. "Adversus Haereses (Book III, Chapter 4)." *The Faith Database.* CD-ROM. Third Millennium Media, 2008.

Stravinskas, Peter M. J. *Our Sunday Visitor's Catholic Encyclopedia.* Huntington, Ind. Our Sunday Visitor Pub., c1991.

Swanson, James. *Dictionary of Biblical Languages with Semantic Domains : Greek (New Testament).* Electronic ed. Oak Harbor: Logos Research Systems, Inc., 1997.

Tertullian. "Against Marcion, Book IV." *The Faith Database.* CD-ROM. Third Millennium Media, 2008.

———. "The Prescription Against Heretics." *The Faith Database.* CD-ROM. Third Millennium Media, 2008.

Thomas Aquinas, Saint; Fathers of the English Dominican Province. *Summa theologica.* Complete English ed. Bellingham, WA: Logos Bible Software, 2009.

Vatican I. "Dogmatic Constitution concerning the Catholic Faith (1798)." ed. Denzinger. *Welcome to the Catholic Church.* CD-ROM. Harmony Media, 2007.

———. "Dogmatic Constitution Concerning the Catholic Faith (1800)." ed. Denzinger. *Welcome to the Catholic Church.* CD-ROM. Harmony Media, 2007.

———. "Dogmatic Constitution on the Catholic Faith." *The Faith Database.* CD-ROM. Third Millennium Media, 2008.

————. "Dogmatic Constitution on the Church of Christ (1836)." ed. Denzinger. *Welcome to the Catholic Church.* CD-ROM. Harmony Media, 2007.

Vaticana, Libreria Editrice. *Catechism of the Catholic Church.* United States Conference of Catholic Bishops, 2011.

Vincent of Lerins. "Commonitory for the Antiquity and Universality of the Catholic Faith." *The Faith Database.* CD-ROM. Third Millennium Media, 2008.

Williamson, Peter. *Catholic Principles for Interpreting Scripture: A Study of the Pontifical Biblical Commission's the Interpretation of the Bible in the Church.* Vol. 22. Roma: Pontificio Istituto Biblico, 2001.

XVI, Pope Benedict. *Jesus of Nazareth: From the Baptism in the Jordan to the Transfiguration.* Ignatius Press, 2008.

About the Author

Hubert M. Sanders Jr. holds a master's degree in theology from Sacred Heart Major Seminary, where he teaches as an adjunct professor.

He also teaches the study of Catholic theology at Brother Rice High School in Bloomfield Hills, Michigan, where he relishes the opportunity to help young people grow in Christ. He's an active member of Presentation Our Lady of Victory Parish in Detroit. Sanders, a widower, has four daughters.